VISUAL QUICKSTART GUIDE

GOOGLE GMAIL

Steve Schwartz

Peachpit Press

Visual QuickStart Guide

Google Gmail

Steve Schwartz

Peachpit Press

1249 Eighth Street
Berkeley, CA 94710
510/524-2178
800/283-9444
510/524-2221 (fax)

Find us on the Web at: www.peachpit.com
To report errors, please send a note to errata@peachpit.com

Peachpit Press is a division of Pearson Education

Editor: Suzie Nasol
Production Coordinator: Myrna Vladic
Compositor: Steve Schwartz
Indexer: FireCrystal Communications
Cover design: Aren Howell, Peachpit Press

ISBN: 0-321-33016-1

9 8 7 6 5 4 3 2 1

Printed and bound in the United States of America

Dedication

To my good friend, Russ

Special Thanks to:

The Peachpit Press editorial and production team for being so helpful and supportive

Table of Contents

INTRODUCTION

Gmail is a free, by invitation only, Web-based email system provided by Google, the most popular search engine on the Internet.

The purpose of this book is to teach you how to use Gmail as a primary or secondary email account. Many people these days ignore their free *ISP* (Internet Service Provider) account because it requires them to learn to use an email client, such as Microsoft Office Outlook, Outlook Express, Apple Mail, or Entourage. Because Gmail is accessible using almost any Windows, Mac, or Linux Web browser, there's less to learn—even new users can quickly master a Web browser.

Gmail also makes an excellent secondary email account. Many users reserve their ISP or corporate email account for business correspondence and staying in touch with close friends. Web-based accounts such as Gmail can be used for site registrations and any correspondence in which there is a high probability of generating spam.

Of course, why you've chosen Gmail and how you intend to use it are up to you. Regardless, I think you'll be pleased with your choice.

System Requirements

Gmail is accessible from any PC, Mac, or Linux computer with Internet access and a supported Web browser. Its display can currently be set for any of 38 languages.

Browser support

According to Google, these browsers and later versions fully support Gmail's *standard view* (see Chapter 2):

- Internet Explorer 5.5 (Windows)
- Netscape 7.1 (Windows, Mac, Linux)
- Mozilla 1.4 (Windows, Mac, Linux)
- Firefox 0.8 (Windows, Mac, Linux)
- Safari 1.2.1 (Mac)

Basic HTML view (see Chapter 2) is supported by these browsers and later versions:

- Internet Explorer 4.0
- Netscape 4.07
- Opera 6.03

You must have cookies enabled in your browser. And if your browser supports it, you should enable JavaScript, too.

✔ Tips

- The current version of Safari for Mac OS X (2.0.2) is *not* fully compatible with Gmail in standard view (**Figure i.1**).
- If you are using Safari 2.0.2, I strongly recommend that you use Gmail's links to navigate among pages rather than clicking the Back button. Doing so can confuse Safari, causing it to go to the first page loaded prior to entering Gmail or forcing it to reload its Java application.

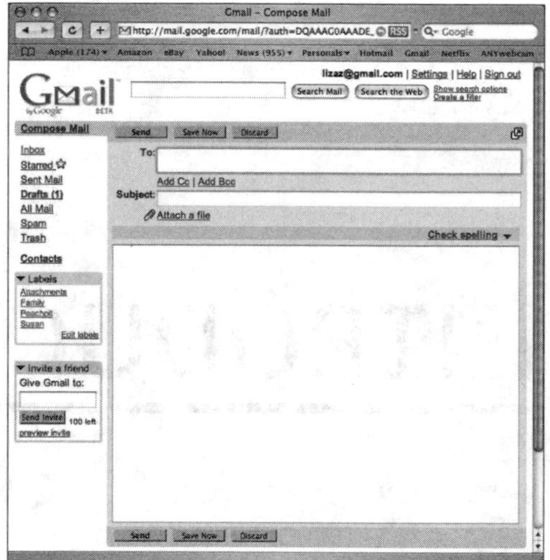

Figure i.1 When composing a letter in Safari 2.0.2, the option to format text is absent. Only plain text (unformatted) email is supported.

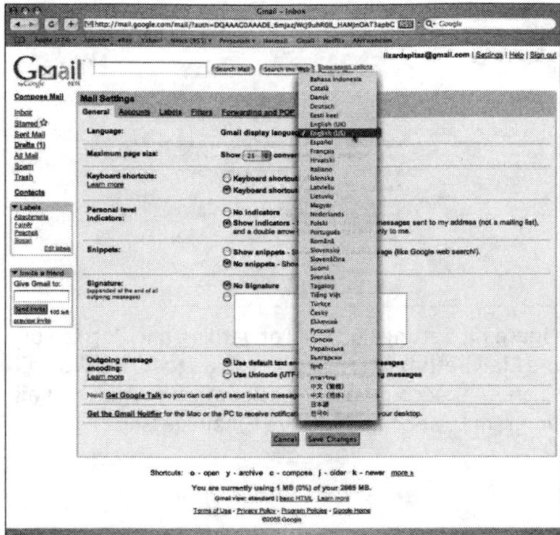

Figure i.2 You can change Gmail's display language by choosing an option from this pop-up menu.

Would you also like to make English (UK) your language for other Google sites?

Yes No

Figure i.3 When changing languages in Gmail, you can opt to use the same new language to display all Google sites.

Language support

Gmail's interface (buttons, links, and dialog boxes) can be displayed in 38 languages.

To set the language for Gmail:

1. Click the Settings link at the top of any Gmail page.
   The Mail Settings page appears.
2. If it isn't already selected, click the link for the General tab.
3. Choose a language from the Gmail display language pop-up menu (**Figure i.2**).
4. Click the Save Changes button.
5. Switching to some languages is accompanied by a dialog box (**Figure i.3**). To use the chosen language to display *all* Google Web sites, click Yes. To retain the language settings you've chosen for other Google sites, click No.

Gmail Benefits

Even if you already have an email account with your *ISP* (Internet Service Provider) or your employer, a Gmail account offers many important benefits:

- Gmail provides more than 2,000 MB (or 2 GB) of disk storage for your messages and attachments. As a result, it's unlikely you'll ever need to delete messages because you're running out of space.
- Gmail doesn't require you to carefully configure and master a separate email program.
- Being browser-based means that you can check for new mail or compose messages on *any* computer—not just the one that contains your email program and account information. Reading your mail is just as simple when you're at work, connected at a coffee house, or on vacation as it is when you're sitting in front of your desktop PC or Mac.
- If you prefer using an email program, you can configure it to work with Gmail. In addition to Web access, Gmail provides *POP* (Post Office Protocol) support (**Figure i.4**). As a result, you can configure your email program to send and receive Gmail. You can also forward incoming Gmail messages to your ISP or corporate email account.
- If you run the standard (Java-based) version of Gmail, it has a feature that distinguishes it from other Web-based email services, such as Hotmail and Yahoo! Instead of relying on an ancillary application to notify you of new email, Gmail automatically checks for mail every two minutes. There's nothing to click or refresh just to see if you've received mail—*it simply appears in the Inbox!*

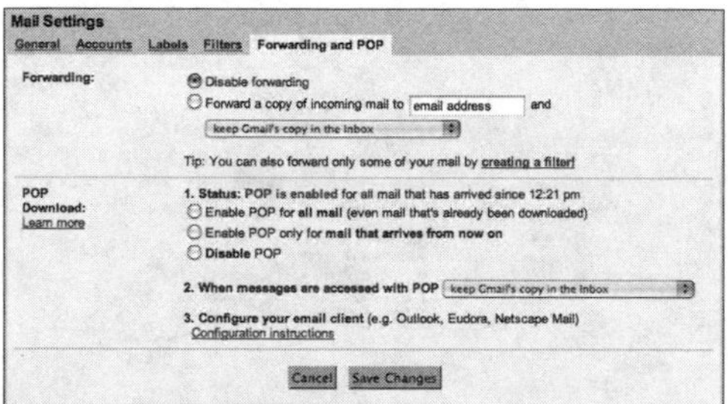

Figure i.4 Settings on the Forwarding and Pop tab of the Mail Settings screen enable you to forward Gmail to another account or to configure your regular email program to send and receive Gmail messages.

Gmail and Google Accounts

https://www.google.com/accounts

Google Accounts is your gateway to all your Google services, such as Google Groups, Froogle Shopping List, and Google Alerts. When you sign in to Google Accounts, you're simultaneously signing in to all your Google services.

If you don't already have a Google Account, signing up for Gmail creates one for you. To sign in to your Google account (at the address above), enter your Gmail user name and password.

When emailing images, use Gmail

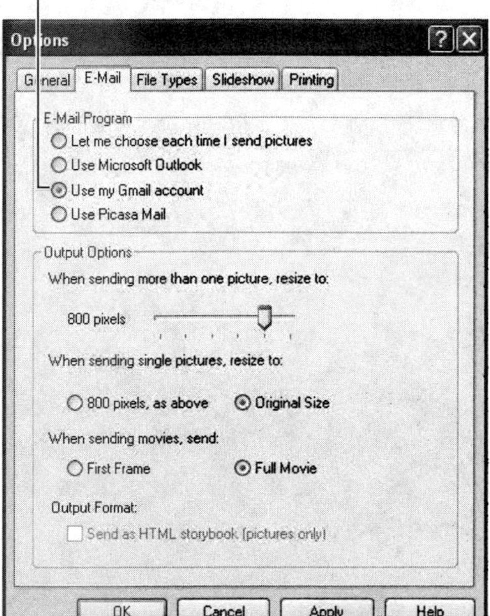

Figure i.5 You can instruct Picasa to use Gmail to email selected photos.

Enhancing Gmail

Google and a host of independent developers offer a variety of free add-ons. They enhance Gmail by providing new features, improving existing ones, or linking to your Gmail account. After you've mastered the Gmail essentials by reading this book, you might want to check out the add-ons. Here are a few of the most interesting ones:

- **Gmail Notifier** (Windows XP or 2000, and Mac OS X 10.3.8 or higher) notifies you of new Gmail, showing the subject, sender, and a snippet of the message. Gmail Notifier is discussed in Chapter 4 (*http://toolbar.google.com/gmail-helper/*).
- **Google Toolbar** (Windows XP or 2000, Mac OS X 10.2 or higher, Red Hat Linux 8.0 or higher) is a toolbar for Firefox and Internet Explorer. It includes a Gmail search button (*http://toolbar.google.com*).
- **Google Talk** (Windows XP or 2000) is a text chat/instant messaging application. (Mac users can connect via iChat.) If you have a microphone and speakers, you can also use it for voice chats. Like Gmail Notifier, Google Talk notifies you of new Gmail messages. You must have a Gmail account in order to use Google Talk (*http://www.google.com/talk/*).
- **Picasa** (Windows XP or 2000) is a full-featured image organizer and editor. The current version (2.1.0) allows you to use your Gmail account (**Figure i.5**) to easily exchange favorite photos with friends and relatives (*http://google.picasa.com*).

  For in-depth information on Picasa, pick up *Organizing and Editing Your Photos with Picasa: Visual QuickProject* (Peachpit Press, 2005).

1

Setting Up a Gmail Account

Before you can begin using Gmail, you must first be invited to create an account. Yes, this is a "by invitation only" party. In this chapter, we'll step through the process of receiving an invitation and creating a Gmail account. In preparation for using the account to send and receive email messages, you'll also set your General Mail Settings.

After you've created an account, you'll learn how to invite others to create their own Gmail accounts. And if you should eventually want to cancel the Gmail service, instructions are provided for that, too.

Creating an Account

At present, you can only create a Gmail account if you're *invited* to do so. A current Gmail user must send you an email invitation (**Figure 1.1**) offering you the opportunity to create an account.

To create a new account:

1. Open the invitation message in your normal email program or Web browser.
2. Click the link near the top of the message.
   If it isn't already running, your browser launches and opens to the Gmail site (**Figure 1.2**).
3. Enter the requested information, and then click the link at the bottom of the page.
   If the user name is available and there are no errors on the page, your new account will be created. Otherwise, make the necessary corrections and try again.
4. To view your Gmail account, click the link on the new Web page that appears.

✔ Tips

- The hardest part of creating an account is finding a user name that isn't already in use. To determine if a name is available, click the Check Availability button. (If the name isn't available and you just click the button at the bottom of the form, you'll have to fill out the form again.)
- A user name must contain at least six characters. Periods can be included, but don't count toward the six.
- Choose your user name carefully. Once created, it cannot be changed.
- Longer passwords are more secure. If you think you can remember it, create one that combines uppercase letters, lowercase letters, and numbers.

```
Steve Schwartz has invited you to open a free Gmail account.

To accept this invitation and register for your account, visit
http://mail.google.com/mail/a-70bd05bace-fea1e19e4d-0b3116158c

Once you create your account, Steve Schwartz will be notified with
your new email address so you can stay in touch with Gmail!

If you haven't already heard about Gmail, it's a new search-based webmail
service that offers:

- Over 2,500 megabytes (two gigabytes) of free storage
- Built-in Google search that instantly finds any message you want
- Automatic arrangement of messages and related replies into
  "conversations"
- Text ads and related pages that are relevant to the content of your
  messages

Gmail is still in an early stage of development. But if you set up an
account, you'll be able to keep it even after we make Gmail more
widely available. We might also ask for your comments and suggestions
periodically and we appreciate your help in making Gmail even better.

Thanks,

The Gmail Team

To learn more about Gmail before registering, visit:
http://mail.google.com/mail/help/benefits.html

(If clicking the URLs in this message does not work, copy and paste them
into the address bar of your browser).
```

Figure 1.1 To respond to the invitation, click the link near the top of the message.

Get started with Gmail

First name: Steven

Last name: Schwartz

Desired Login Name: SSchwartz.VQS @gmail.com
Examples: JSmith, John.Smith
check availability!

Choose a password : •••••••• Password strength: Strong
Minimum of 6 characters in length.

Re-enter password: ••••••••

Security Question: Write my own question
mother's maiden name
If you forget your password we will ask for the answer to your security question. Learn More

Answer: Brill

Secondary email:
This address is used to authenticate your account should you ever encounter problems or forget your password. If you do not have another email address, you may leave this field blank. Learn More

Word Verification: Type the characters you see in the picture below.
eysmeos
eysmeos
characters are not case-sensitive

By registering for the Gmail service, I represent and warrant that I (or, if I am under 18, my legal guardian) understand and agree to the Gmail Terms of Use above. View the Terms of Use , Program Policy and Privacy Policy .
You must accept the Terms of Use to create a Gmail account

I have read and agree to the Terms of Use. Create my account.

Figure 1.2 Fill in the new account form and click the button at the bottom.

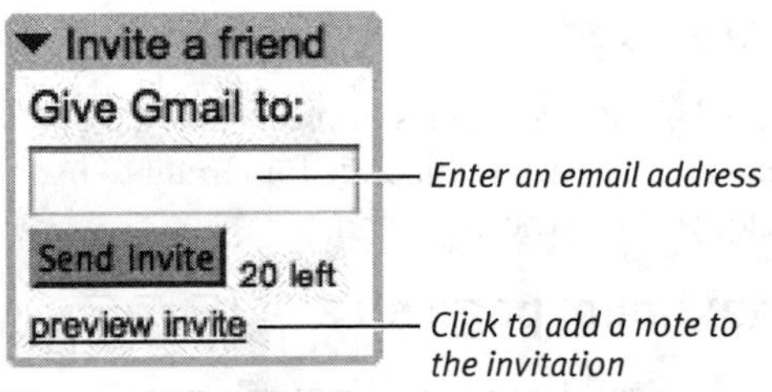

Figure 1.3 Offer a Gmail account to a friend.

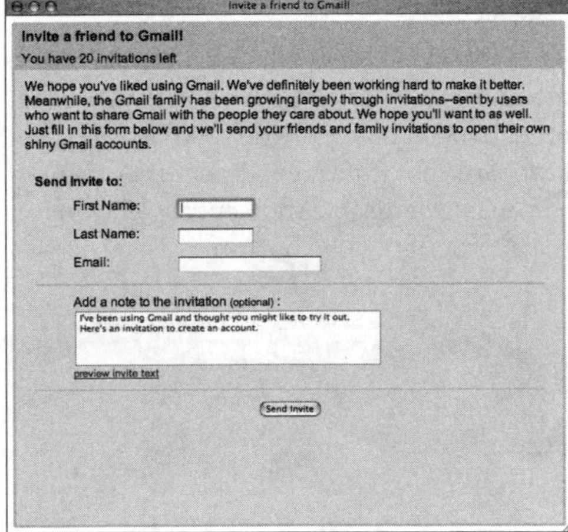

Figure 1.4 If your friend isn't expecting a Gmail invitation, you can use this form to add a personal note.

Steven Schwartz has accepted your invitation to Gmail Inbox
Gmail Team <gmail-noreply@google.com> to me More options Oct 31 (14 hours ago)
Steven Schwartz has accepted your invitation to Gmail and has chosen the brand new address sschwartz@gmail.com. Be one of the first to email Steven at this new Gmail address--just hit reply and send Steven a message. sschwartz@gmail.com has also been automatically added to your contact list so you can stay in touch with Gmail.
Thanks,
The Gmail Team
Reply Forward

Figure 1.5 If the person creates a Gmail account in response to your invitation, the Gmail team will notify you by email.

Inviting Others to Join

Once you have a Gmail account, you can invite others to join, too.

To send an invitation:

1. Open Gmail in your browser by going to *http://mail.google.com*. The Invite a friend box (**Figure 1.3**) can be found on the left side of the browser window.
2. *Do either of the following:*
   - ▲ Type or paste your friend's email address into the box and click Send Invite.

     A standard invitation will be emailed to your friend or associate.
   - ▲ Click the *preview invite* link (see Figure 1.3). The Invite a friend to Gmail window appears (**Figure 1.4**). Fill in the blanks, add a personal note, and click Send Invite.

   If your friend accepts the invitation and creates a Gmail account, you'll receive a confirmation in your Inbox (**Figure 1.5**).

✔ Tips

- ■ Although you may be eager to invite friends to create Gmail accounts, Gmail may not be ready for you. The Invite a friend box may not appear until after you've used Gmail for a while.
- ■ The number of invitations available to you can vary. On the new account created for this book, I started with 20 invitations (see Figure 1.3). On my slightly older Gmail account, I was given 100.

Setting General Preferences

Most Gmail preferences (called *mail settings*) can be modified on an as-needed basis—when or if you get around to it. However, settings on the General tab (**Figure 1.6**) affect your basic interactions with Gmail and can be set immediately.

To view or modify General Mail Settings, click the Settings link in the upper-right corner of the Gmail window. After making changes, click the Save Changes button at the bottom of the page.

Language

The default language is *English (US)*. To specify a different language for Gmail to use, select it from the pop-up list.

Maximum page size

You can set the maximum number of conversations displayed per page to 25, 50, or 100 by selecting an option from this pop-up list.

Keyboard shortcuts

Since Gmail is browser-based, it doesn't have menus like a standalone email client. On the other hand, it *does* provide a variety of keyboard shortcuts (see Appendix A). You can enable or disable shortcuts by clicking the appropriate radio button.

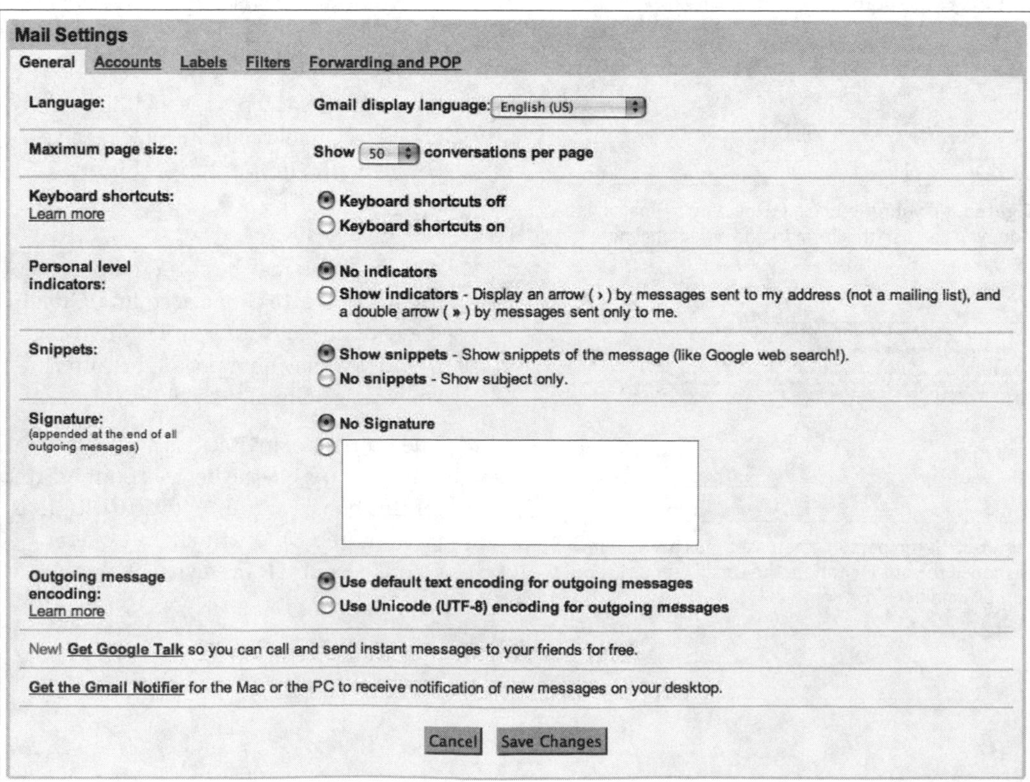

Figure 1.6 The General Mail Settings.

Figure 1.7 Level indicators show whether a given message had multiple recipients or a single recipient.

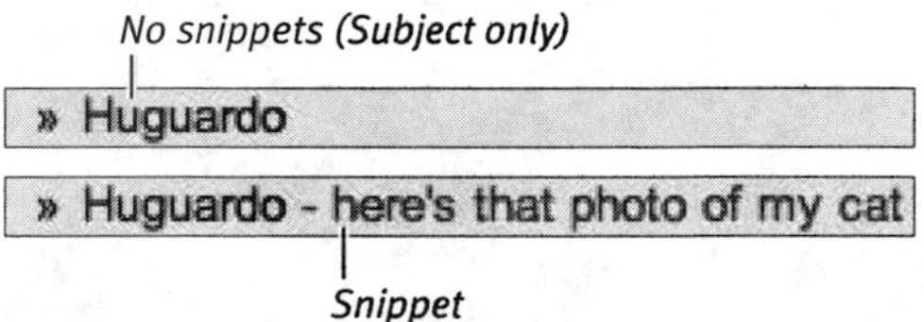

Figure 1.8 If you occasionally have a hard time telling what a message contains by checking its Subject, you may want to enable snippets.

Figure 1.9 Create your email signature in this text box.

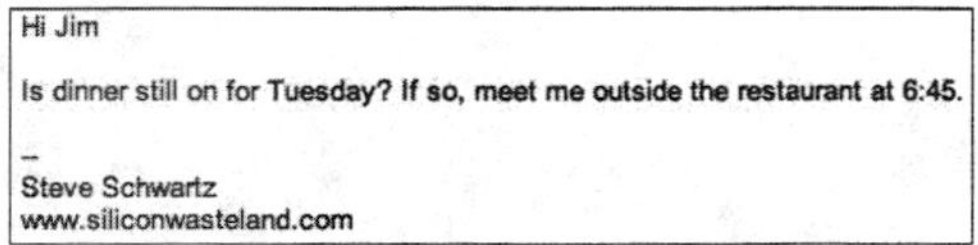

Figure 1.10 Your signature is appended to the end of each new message. You can eliminate the signature from certain messages by deleting it from the text.

Personal level indicators

Level indicators (**Figure 1.7**) provide a way for you to distinguish messages sent only to you from those with multiple recipients.

When enabled, the Subject line of a message addressed only to you is preceded by a double arrow symbol (»), a message with multiple recipients is preceded by a single arrow (›), and a message from a mailing list isn't marked with an arrow. These conventions are applied to outgoing messages, too.

Snippets

When *snippets* (**Figure 1.8**) are enabled, a little of the message text is displayed in the message list (in addition to the Subject). When snippets are disabled, only the Subject is shown.

Signature

A *signature* is one or more lines of text that is appended to every outgoing message (similar to a letter's closing). You can create a traditional signature consisting of name, organization, and/or Web site or one that's thought provoking or funny.

To create a signature, type it in the text box (**Figure 1.9**). For a multi-line signature, press Return/Enter after every line except the last. When the Signature setting is enabled, this signature is added as the final message line or lines (**Figure 1.10**).

Outgoing message encoding

Unless recipients report problems reading the messages you've created in Gmail, select Use default text encoding for outgoing messages.

Cancelling a Gmail Account

If you decide to close your Gmail account, you can do so by following these steps.

1. Click the Settings text link at the top of any Gmail Web page.
2. Click the Accounts tab, and then click the Google Account settings text link.

   A new page opens, displaying your account summary information.
3. In the Delete Account section on the left side of the page, click Delete Gmail Service.

   The Delete Gmail Service page appears (**Figure 1.11**).
4. If you still want Google to be able to contact you, enter a working email address in the New Email Address box.
5. Enter your Gmail password in the Current password box (if it isn't already entered).
6. Click Yes, I want to remove Gmail from my account, and click Remove Gmail.

✔ Tips

- Prior to closing the account, you may wish to send copies of the messages to another email account.
- See the Introduction for a discussion of Google Accounts. (Gmail is only one of several accounts you might have with Google. Cancelling your Gmail account does not affect any other Google services you might have.)

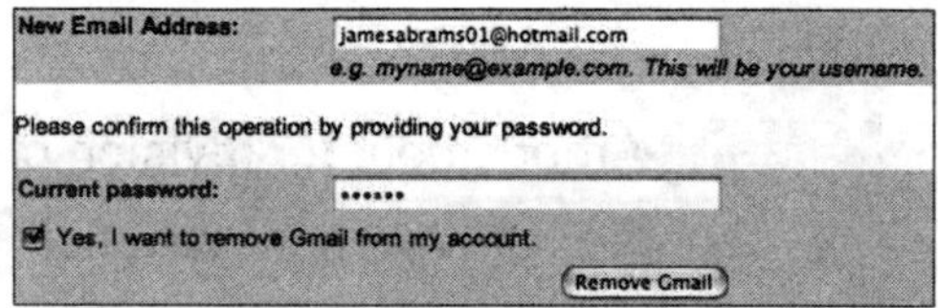

Figure 1.11 If you're no longer interested in using Gmail, you can close your account.

2

GMAIL ESSENTIALS

Now that you've created an account, it's time to learn the basics of using Gmail. In this chapter, you'll learn about:

- Signing in and out of your Gmail account
- The differences between standard and basic view
- The elements of the Gmail interface and how to use them
- Important Gmail terms

Signing In

Unless you've instructed Gmail to Remember me on this computer (**Figure 2.1**), you'll be asked to sign in to your account each time you visit the Gmail Web site.

Figure 2.1 To log in to your Gmail account, enter your user name and password, and click Sign in.

To sign in to your Gmail account:

1. Launch your Web browser and enter any of the following URLs in the Address box:
   - http://mail.google.com/mail/
   - http://mail.google.com
   - http://gmail.google.com
   - http://www.gmail.com
   - http://gmail.com

   These addresses all resolve to the first one.
2. If you have not clicked the Remember me on this computer check box, you will be asked to sign in. Enter your user name (the part of your Gmail address that precedes *@gmail.com*) and your Gmail password. Then click Sign in.

✔ Tips

- In most browsers, you can even skip the *http://* part of the Gmail Web address.
- Clicking Remember me on this computer causes Gmail to store a cookie on your computer that expires in two weeks. As long as you don't sign out of your account, future sign-ins will be automatic.
- You'll note that the sign-in always occurs on a *secure* Web page; that is, the URL begins with https:// rather than http://. If you'd like an entire *session* to be secure, go to *https://gmail.google.com* rather than the addresses listed in Step 1.

Settings | Help | Sign out

Figure 2.2 To end a session and log out of your account, click the Sign out link in the upper-right corner of any Gmail page.

Ending a Gmail Session

You can sign out at the end of a session or simply leave the Gmail site (by closing the browser or visiting a different site).

To end a Gmail session:

- *Do one of the following:*
  - On any Gmail page, click Sign out (**Figure 2.2**). You'll be asked to sign in again at the start of your next session.
  - Quit your browser or go to a non-Gmail Web page. If you clicked Remember me on this computer, you'll bypass the sign-in on subsequent sessions.

✔ Tip

- If your computer isn't in a secure location, the best ways to ensure that no one can access your account is to leave Remember me on this computer unchecked, sign out at the end of every session, and use the secure https:// address to begin each session. (You can store the secure address as a browser *bookmark* or *favorite.*)

Standard vs. Basic View

Gmail is available in two versions: standard and basic. *Standard view* (**Figure 2.3**) is the full Gmail implementation. Because it is Java-based, standard has special features such as the ability to automatically check for new email, respond to keyboard shortcuts, and create formatted email messages. And because of this feature set, you'll normally want to use the standard version—at least whenever you're using a compatible browser.

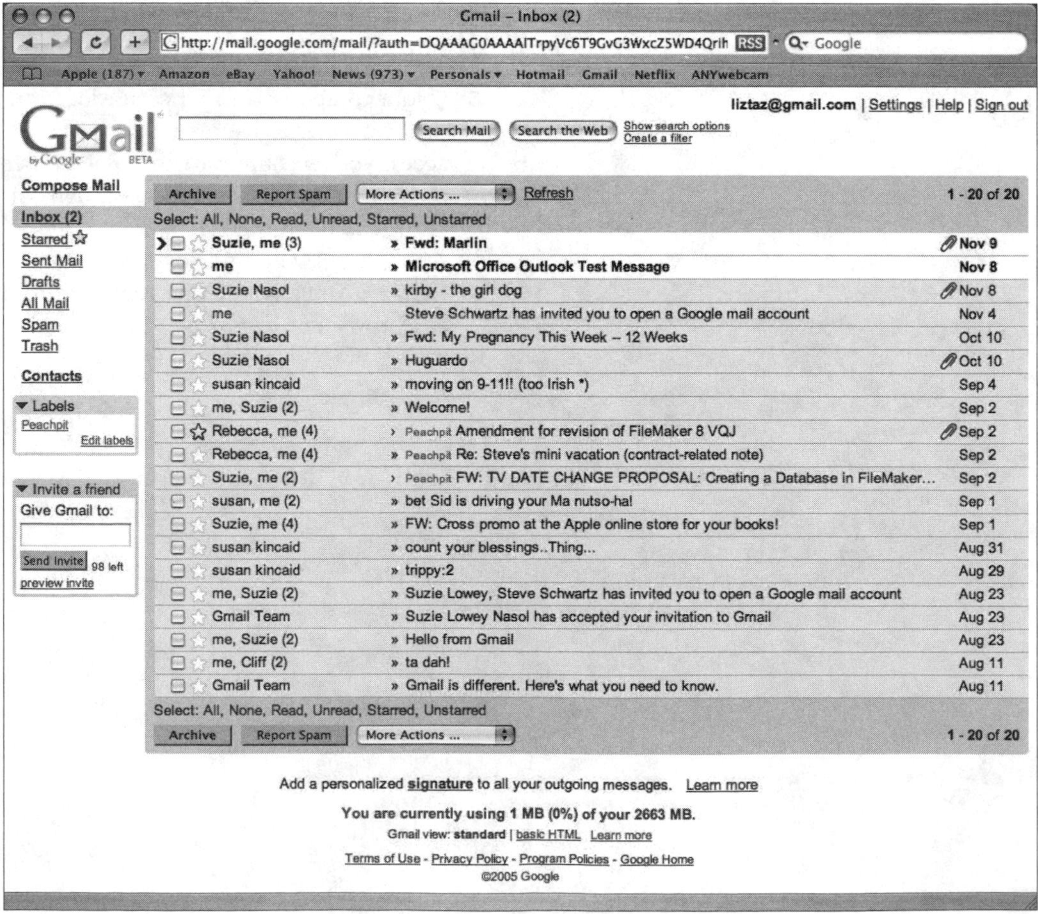

Figure 2.3 In standard view, you have access to all of Gmail's features.

Figure 2.4 Basic view looks similar to standard view, but has a reduced feature set. The orange banner across the top reminds you that you're in basic view.

Basic view (**Figure 2.4**) is created entirely in *HTML* (HyperText Markup Language), the language used to design Web pages. While this version is sufficient for occasional light use (reading new mail, for example), you're unlikely to want to use it as your primary method of interacting with Gmail. Although the interface is similar in the two versions, basic is missing many important—in some respects, critical—features. In basic, you can't:

- Change Gmail preferences (called *settings*)
- Compose formatted email messages (only plain text messages are supported)
- Create message filters
- Add, edit, delete, or import contacts
- Use the spelling checker or keyboard shortcuts

To select a view, click a Gmail view link (standard or basic HTML) at the bottom of any Gmail Web page.

✔ Tips

- If Gmail detects you are using an unsupported browser or that Java isn't enabled, it automatically switches to basic view.
- To switch back from basic to standard view, you can also click the Switch to standard view link in the banner at the top of the Web page (see Figure 2.4).

The Gmail Interface

The Gmail pages contain many elements you will use to interact with Gmail (**Figure 2.5**):

❶ **Search box.** To find one or more messages, enter a text string in the box and click Search Mail. You can search for a person's name or email address, as well as words in the Subject or the message text (see Chapter 7).

❷ **Search the Web.** Click this button to perform a Google search of the Web, based on the contents of the search box.

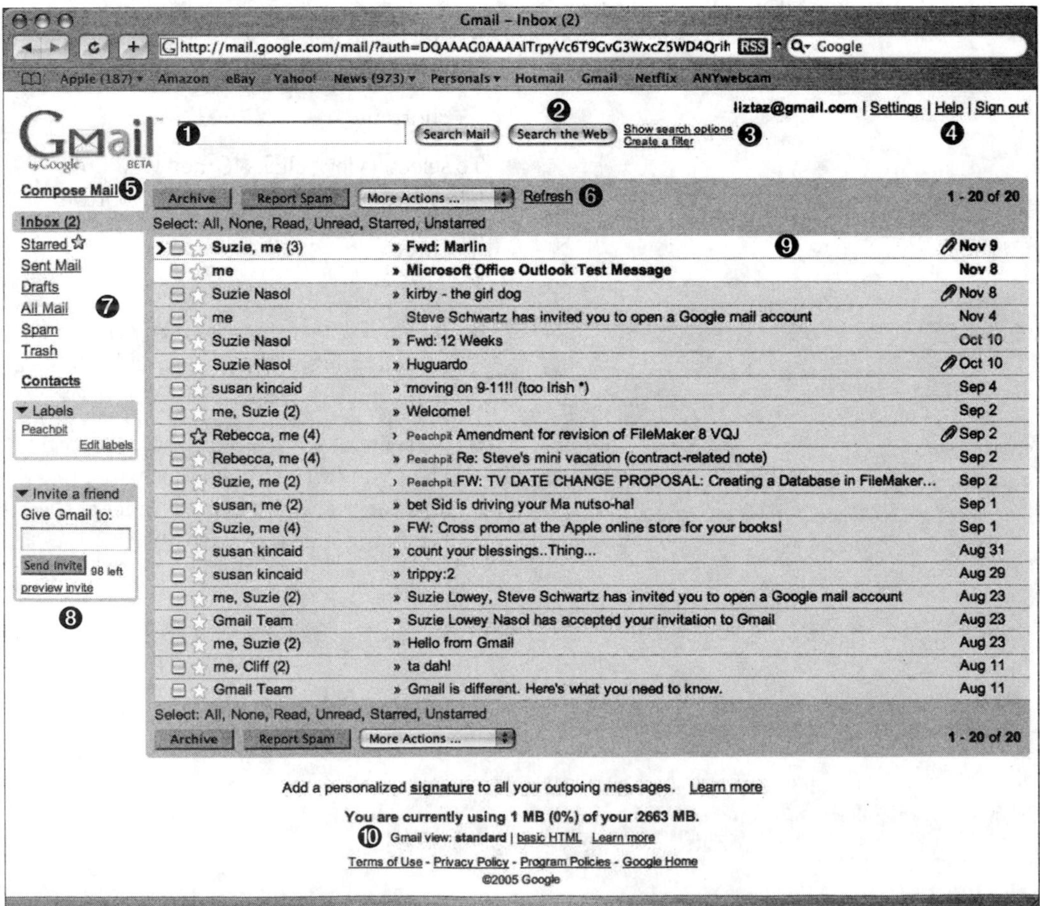

Figure 2.5 The Gmail interface (standard view).

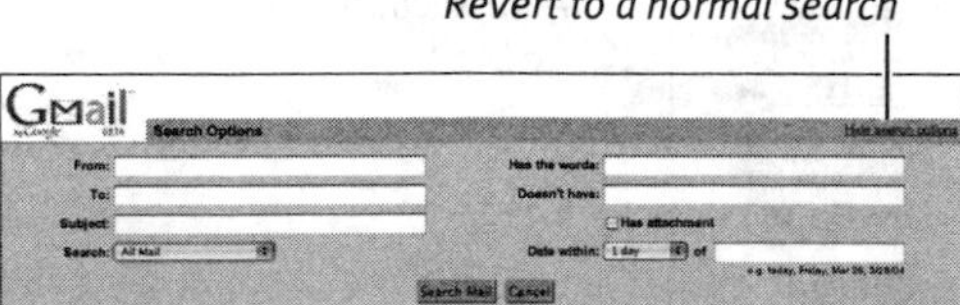

Figure 2.6 With the search options revealed, it's easy to perform a more specific search.

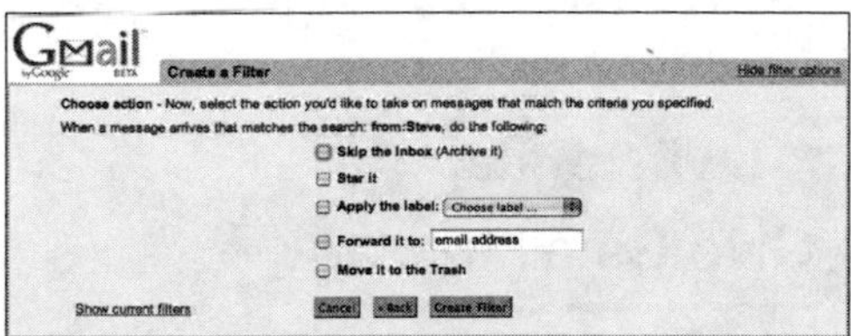

Figure 2.7 You can create filters to automatically manage your incoming mail.

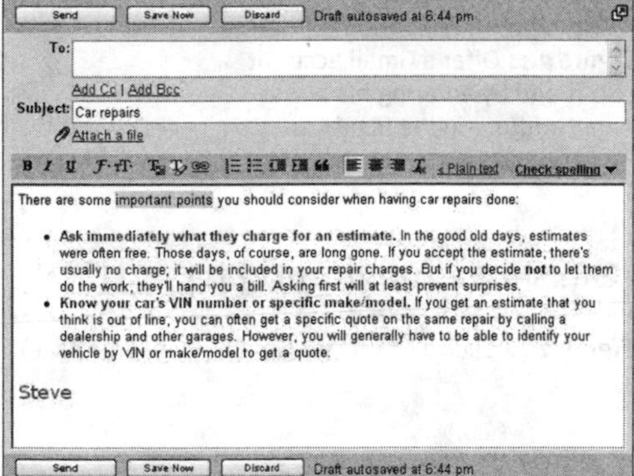

Figure 2.8 You can format Gmail messages to include multiple fonts, sizes, styles, colors, and bulleted or numbered points.

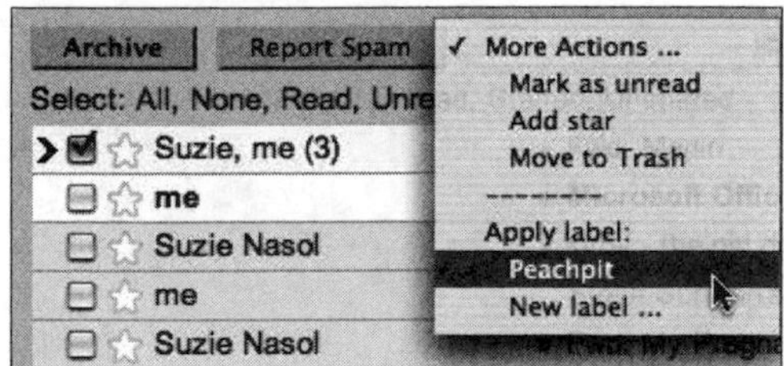

Figure 2.9 The More Actions drop-down menu.

❸ **Show search options.** To perform an *advanced search* (restricting the search to specific message components, a date range, or a message class, for example), click Show search options (**Figure 2.6**). Another way to perform such a search is to type *advanced search operators* into the search box (see Appendix B).

Create a filter. A *filter* (see Chapter 7) is similar to a message rule in Microsoft email programs. By applying a filter's criteria, incoming messages can be archived, moved to the Trash, or have a label or star applied to them. To create a new filter, click Create a filter (**Figure 2.7**).

❹ **Settings.** To set Gmail preferences, click the Settings link.

Help. Gmail Help is a series of Web pages with embedded links to related help topics. Click Help to open the main Help page.

Sign out. Click Sign out to securely end a Gmail session. The next time you visit the Gmail site, you'll be prompted for your user name and password.

❺ **Compose Mail.** Click this link to create a new email message. In most browsers, messages can contain formatting, such as multiple fonts, font styles, and colors (**Figure 2.8**).

❻ **Buttons.** At the top and repeated on the bottom of most Gmail pages are one or more buttons. (The buttons vary according to the message list displayed.) Click a button to perform the specified action on the current message or on all *selected messages* (ones that are checked).

More Actions. Click this drop-down menu (**Figure 2.9**) to choose an action to perform on the current message or on all selected messages.

continues on next page

❼ **Section links.** Click links in this area to go to a specific Gmail section. These links are the equivalent of folders in other email programs. The current section is highlighted in blue (**Figure 2.10**).

❽ **Invite a friend.** New Gmail accounts can only be created in response to an *invitation* from another Gmail user (**Figure 2.11**). To extend an invitation to a colleague, friend, or relative, enter the person's email address and click Send Invite. (See Chapter 1 for more information.)

❾ **Message list.** Every Gmail section (such as the Inbox, Sent Mail, Spam, and Trash) has an area in which its message list is displayed. To read a message, click the message header. To perform an action on one or more messages, select the messages by clicking their check boxes. Then specify an action by clicking a button above or beneath the message list, or choose an action from the More Actions drop-down menu.

❿ **Gmail view.** By clicking one of these two links (**Figure 2.12**), you can switch between *standard view* (for Java-enabled compatible browsers) and *basic view* (for incompatible browsers or those without Java support).

Standard view relies on a Java program to check for new mail every two minutes and support advanced functions, such as the spelling checker and the ability to create formatted messages. Basic view is created entirely from HTML.

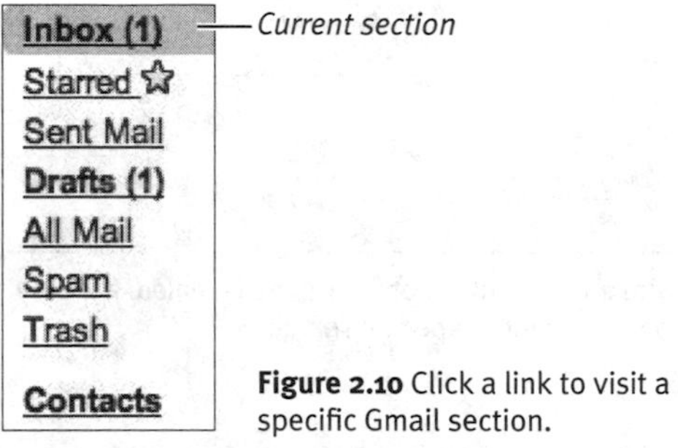

Figure 2.10 Click a link to visit a specific Gmail section.

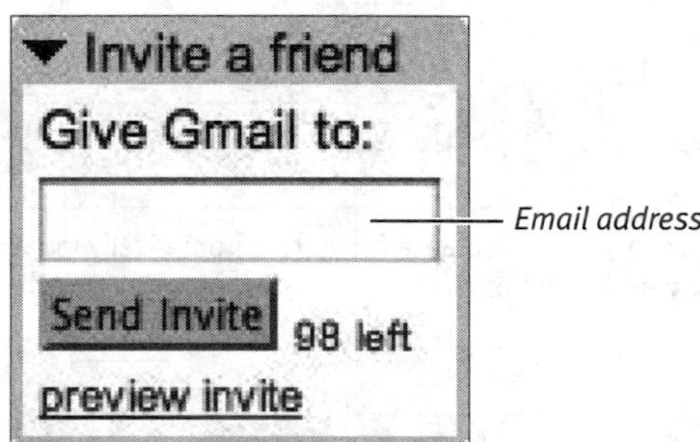

Figure 2.11 Offer a Gmail account to a friend by entering his or her email address in the text box.

Gmail view: **standard** | basic HTML

Figure 2.12 Click a link to set Gmail's view (interface).

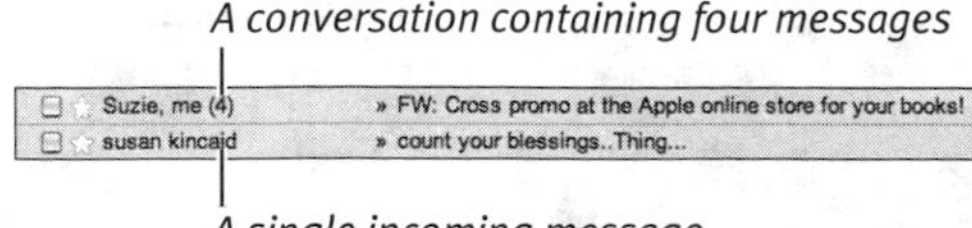

Figure 2.13 A conversation is denoted by a number in parentheses, showing the number of messages.

bet Sid is driving your Ma nutso-ha! Inbox Susan

susan kincaid Well, haven't heard anything back from you. (May... Sep 1

Steve Schwartz to susan More options Sep 2

Having a WONDERFUL time here. I'm happy to say that this is unquestionably the BEST thing I've done for my personal life in the past four years. I think we have a winner here! :-)

Glad to hear about the rental and your ability to keep Thing. It really is wonderful that the landlord saw his way to clear to make this situation a teensy bit more palatable for you.

- Show quoted text -

Reply Forward

Figure 2.14 When you open a conversation, the messages are presented in a stack. The newest message (at the bottom of the stack) is displayed. You can view any message in the conversation by clicking its header.

Gmail Conventions

Gmail uses terms for some of its components that you might not immediately understand. This section explains the ones that are most important for you to know.

Inbox. In other email applications, the Inbox is where your incoming email is stored. While this is also the case in Gmail, other messages are stored there, too (see *Conversation*).

Conversation. When you or a recipient reply to an email, the messages are grouped to make them more convenient to locate and read. A conversation consists of two or more messages: an original and a reply. As long as each of you writes every response as an email *reply*, Gmail will treat the messages as a conversation.

Conversations can occur in any Gmail section, such as the Inbox, Sent Mail, or Starred. When a message is part of a conversation, the participants' names are followed by a number in parentheses (**Figure 2.13**). The number denotes the number of messages in the conversation. To read a conversation (**Figure 2.14**), click its header.

All Mail. The All Mail page contains headers for all Gmail messages you have sent or received. Only deleted messages aren't listed. Although Gmail provides 2 GB of storage per account, your Inbox and Sent Mail can become littered with messages over time. You can eliminate some of this clutter by *archiving* less important and older messages. Once archived, the messages are removed from their original page (such as the Inbox). They can then be viewed on the All Mail page.

continues on next page

Spam. This Gmail section is the equivalent of a Junk Mail folder in other email programs. Messages that Gmail suspects of being *spam* (unwanted, unsolicited email) are stored here. If Gmail misses one, you can mark a received message as being spam by selecting the message and clicking the Report Spam button.

Filters. You can automate the handling of incoming mail by creating message rules called *filters*. When a new message meets a filter's criteria, the filter's actions are applied to the message (**Figure 2.15**).

Labels. Labels are the equivalent of mail folders in other email programs. By assigning a label to certain messages (such as *Dogs* or *Budget Assignment*), those messages and conversations are listed in a separate label message list. Labels can be applied manually or be the result of a filter action. To view messages with a particular label, click the label's name on the left side of any message list (**Figure 2.16**).

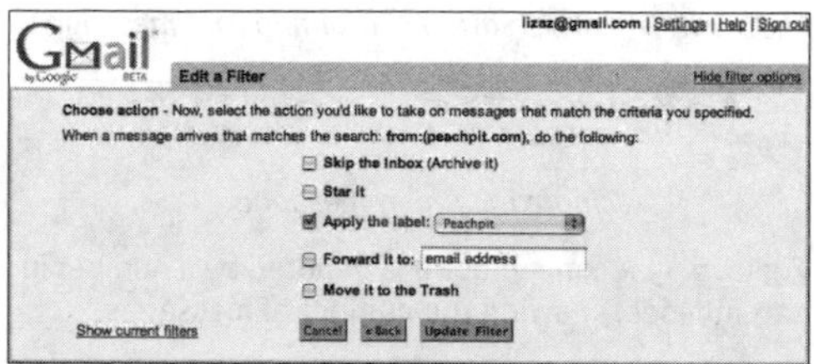

Figure 2.15 A filter can perform any of the actions shown here.

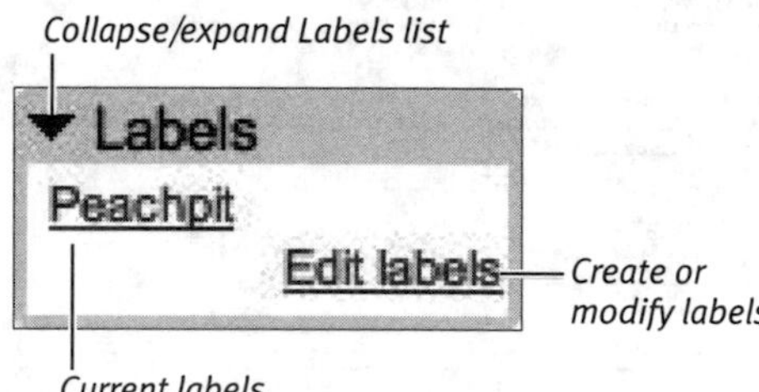

Figure 2.16 To view messages that have been assigned to a label, click its name. To create a new label, modify an existing label, or delete a label, click Edit labels.

Help Center. Help for Gmail is provided as a series of Web pages (**Figure 2.17**). When you click the Help link at the top of any page, the Help Center page opens in a new window. To view a help topic, click its link. To search the Help Center for all references to a topic, enter a search word or phrase in the Search Help Center box and then click the Search button.

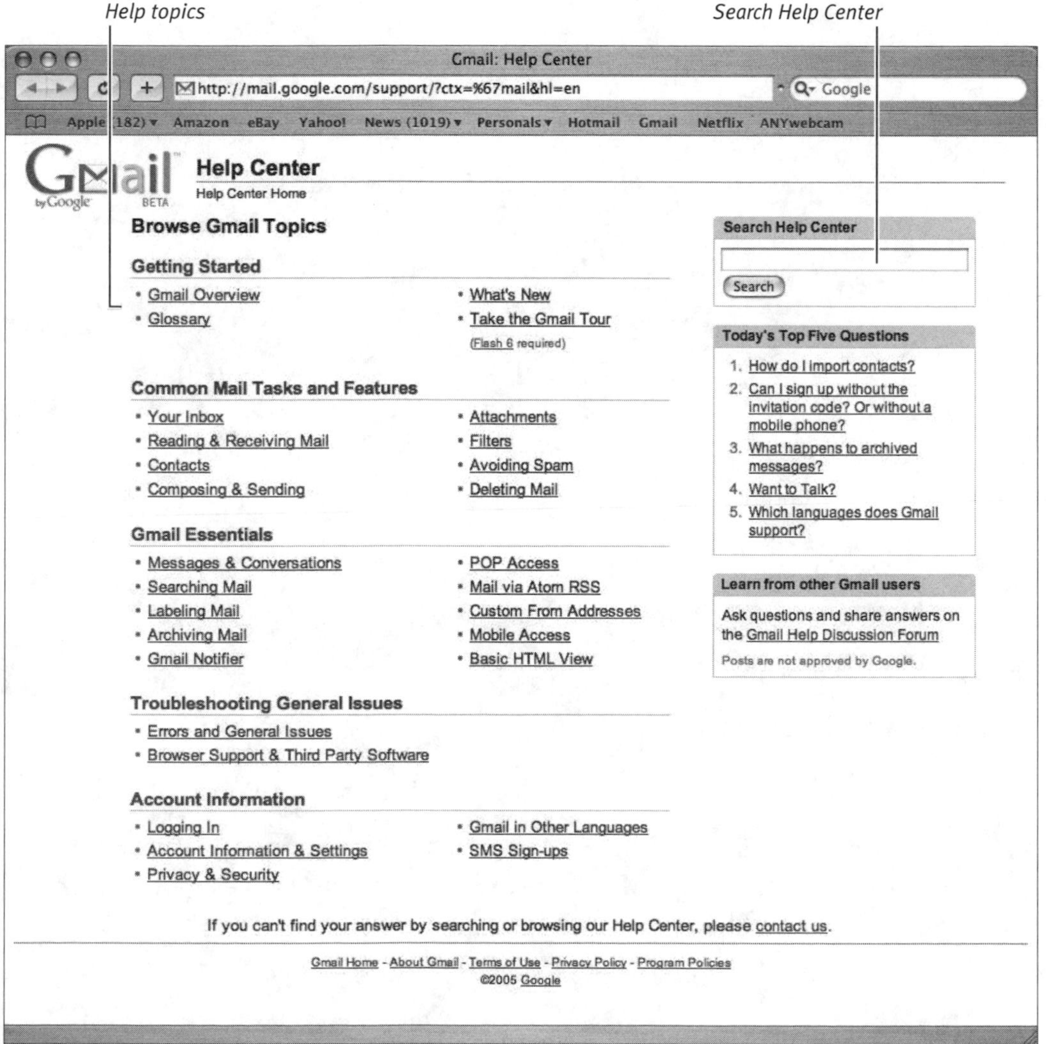

Figure 2.17 Click links in the Help Center to learn more about Gmail.

3

Working with Contacts

The Contacts section of your Gmail account serves the same purpose as the *address book* in other email programs. It's the repository of your stored Gmail contact records. A contact record can consist of as little as an email address, but typically contains the person or company's name, too. Optionally, a contact record can include other information, such as a street address, phone number, and alternate email addresses, for example.

Whenever you use Gmail to send mail to someone new, the recipient's email address is automatically stored in Contacts as a new record. And when you address a message by typing an email address in the To, Cc, or Bcc box, Gmail consults your Contacts and displays a drop-down list of matching people and addresses.

This chapter explains how to create and manage records in Contacts. For information on using your contacts to address messages, see Chapter 5.

Adding Contacts

In addition to automatically creating contacts by emailing people and companies, you can manually create new contact records.

To create a new contact record:

1. Click the Contacts link on the left side of any Gmail page.
2. On the Contacts page, click the Add Contact link.
3. On the Add Contact page (**Figure 3.1**). enter a display name for the contact in the Name box, such as Susan Jones or Anacom Technical Support.
4. Enter the person or company's email address in the Primary Email box.
5. If that's all the information you want to enter for this contact, click Save. Otherwise, continue with Step 6.
6. To add more detailed information for the contact, click add more contact info.

   The pane expands and presents two new sections: Personal and Work (**Figure 3.2**).
7. Enter the additional data.

   You can rename the section heads (by typing over them), select other field labels from the pop-up lists, or add more sections by clicking the add section link.
8. When you're finished, click Save.

   The saved data for the contact is shown.

✔ Tips

- To add fields to a section, click the add another field link. To delete an unnecessary section, click remove section link.
- To create a new contact from a received message, open the message, click More options, and then click Add sender to Contacts list.

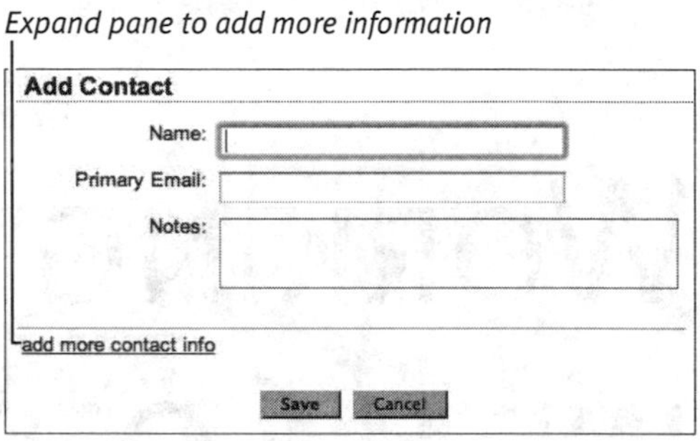

Expand pane to add more information

Figure 3.1 At a minimum, enter a name and email address for the new contact.

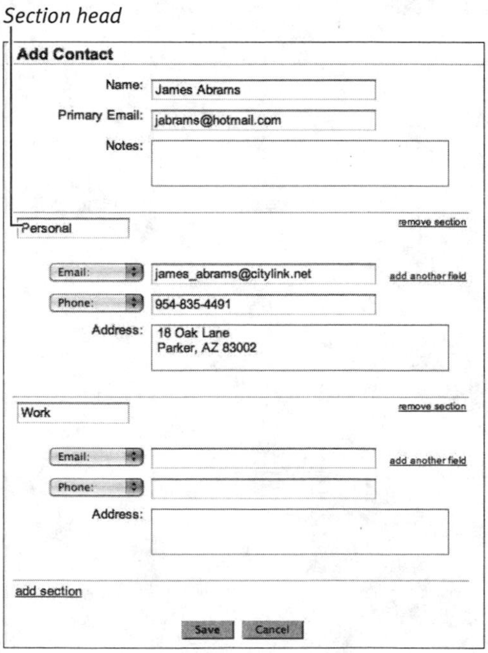

Section head

Figure 3.2 You can record additional information (organized into sections) for any contact.

Edit this contact record

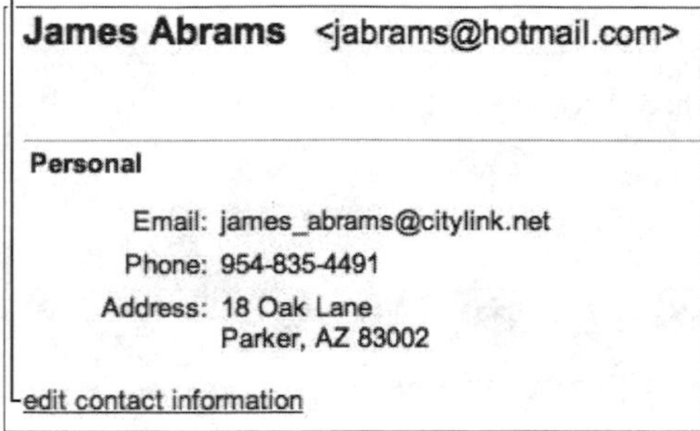

Figure 3.3 The current information for the selected contact is displayed.

Edit Contact
Name: James Abrams
Primary Email: jabrams@hotmail.com
Notes:
Personal
remove section
Email: james_abrams@citylink.net
add another field
Phone: 954-835-4491
IM: jabrams43 (Yahoo Messenger)
Address: 18 Oak Lane
Parker, AZ 83002
add more contact info
Save Cancel

Figure 3.4 Use the Edit Contact page in the same manner as described for the Add Contact page. Click Save when you're finished editing.

Editing Contacts

Information for a contact can change at any time. For instance, people move and change internet providers. Or you may just pick up an additional bit of data that isn't currently part of the person's contact record. You can edit contact records whenever you wish.

To edit contact information:

1. Click the Contacts link on the left side of any Gmail page.
2. On the Contacts page, locate the contact you want to edit by doing one of the following:
   - ▲ Click the Frequently Mailed link to display only contacts with whom you regularly correspond. Or click All Contacts to view your complete contact list.
   - ▲ Search for the contact by entering part of his/her name or email address in the Search Contacts box. Then click the Search Contacts button.
3. Click any part of the contact (the name or email address).

   The current data for the person or company is shown (**Figure 3.3**).
4. Click the edit contact information link.
5. On the Edit Contact page (**Figure 3.4**), make any desired changes, and click Save.

✔ Tips

- To learn more about searching for contacts, see "Searching for Contacts," later in this chapter.
- You must be in Gmail's *standard view* to add, edit, delete, or import contacts.

Deleting Contacts

You can delete contacts that you no longer need. In addition to purging dead email addresses, you can eliminate contact records that were automatically created by Gmail. (Whenever you email someone new, Gmail creates a contact record for that address. Although this is a simple way to build the Contacts list, it can also create some contact records that you probably won't use again.)

To delete contact records:

1. Click the Contacts link on the left side of any Gmail page.
2. On the Contacts page, locate the contact or contacts you want to delete. You can click the Frequently Mailed link to display only contacts with whom you regularly correspond, or click All Contacts to view the complete contact list.
3. Click the check box of each contact you want to delete (**Figure 3.5**).
4. Click the Delete button.

   The selected contact records are deleted.

✔ Tips

- Deleting a contact record is irreversible; you cannot undo a deletion.
- The Delete button is also available while viewing or editing a contact record (**Figure 3.6**).
- To delete *all* contacts, scroll to the bottom of the Contacts page, click the All link (**Figure 3.7**) to select all contacts, and then click Delete.

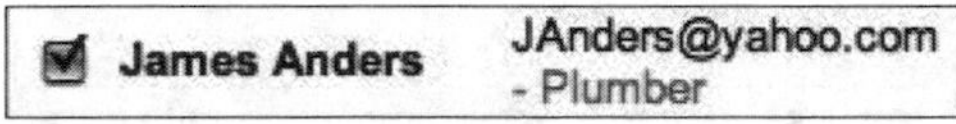

Figure 3.5 Mark contacts for deletion by clicking their check box in the Contacts list.

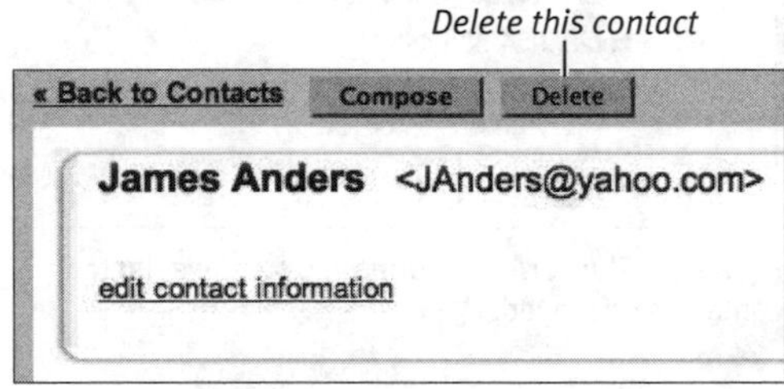

Figure 3.6 You can also delete a contact while viewing or editing it.

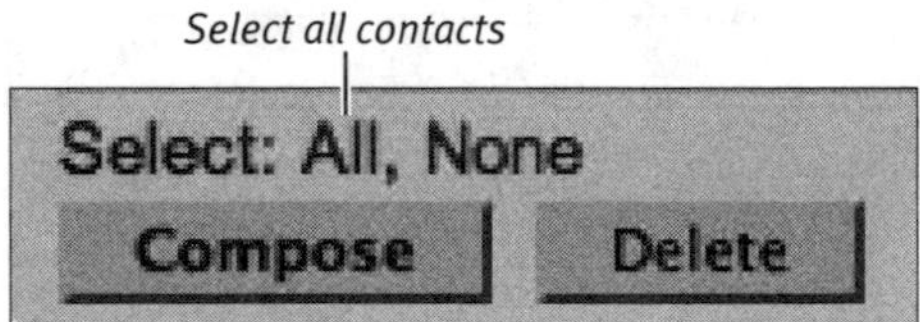

Figure 3.7 To delete all contact records, click All to select all records and then click Delete.

apple computer [Search Contacts]

Figure 3.8 Enter search text in the box and click the Search Contacts button.

Searching for Contacts

If you've been using Gmail for a long time or you have imported an address book from another email program (see "Importing Contacts," in the next section), finding a contact by scrolling through the list can be impractical. Similarly, finding multiple contacts that have something in common (employees of the same company, for instance) can also be cumbersome. The solution to either problem is to *search* for the contact or contacts.

To search for contacts:

1. Click the Contacts link on the left side of any Gmail page.
2. Enter a search string in the box above the Contacts list (**Figure 3.8**), and click Search Contacts.

   A list of all matching contacts is displayed.

✔ Tips

- You can use whole or partial words as search text. Capitalization is ignored.
- You can search for *any* text in a contact record. For example, to find only local contacts, you might use your area code, ZIP code, or city as the search text.
- To delete multiple contacts that share something in common (such as a company name or Internet domain), search for the common element, click the All link, and then click Delete.
- After a search, click the Frequently Mailed or All Contacts link to restore the full contact list.
- It isn't necessary to restore the Contacts list before conducting another search. Searches always operate on *all* contact records—not just the visible ones.

Importing Contacts

If Gmail isn't your first email client, you probably have an address book from another program or a browser-based client. If the address book can be exported or saved as a *CSV* (Comma Separated Values) file, the data can be imported into Gmail's Contacts. After creating the export file (as explained on the following pages), perform the steps on this page to import the data into Gmail.

Gmail's import procedure is extremely flexible. The fields in the exported address book can be in any order, and contact names can be in a single field or multiple fields (such as First, Middle, and Last). Note, however, that the exported data *must* begin with a header record that lists the field names.

If your other email program can't generate a CSV file, you can use a spreadsheet program (Excel, for example) to create the data file from scratch. Or you can export the contacts in another format (such as tab-delimited) and resave them as a CSV file in your spreadsheet program.

To import contact data into Gmail:

1. Click the Contacts link on the left side of any Gmail page.
2. Click the Import link.

   The Import Contacts window opens (**Figure 3.9**).
3. To select your data file, click Choose File (Mac) or Browse (Windows).

   A file dialog box appears (**Figure 3.10**).
4. Select your CSV file, and then click Choose (Mac) or Open (Windows).
5. Click the Import Contacts button.

   The data is imported into Gmail, creating new contact records.

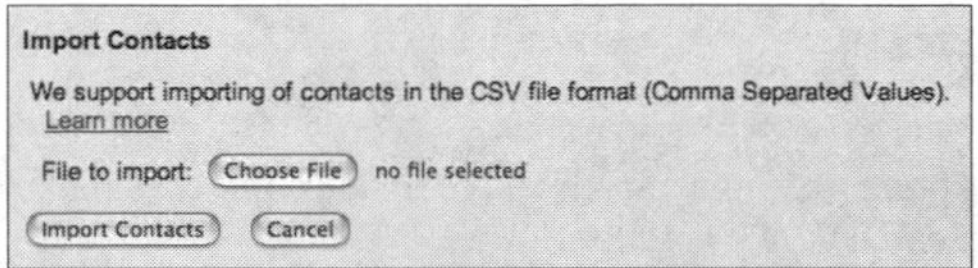

Figure 3.9 Locate the CSV file and then click Import Contacts.

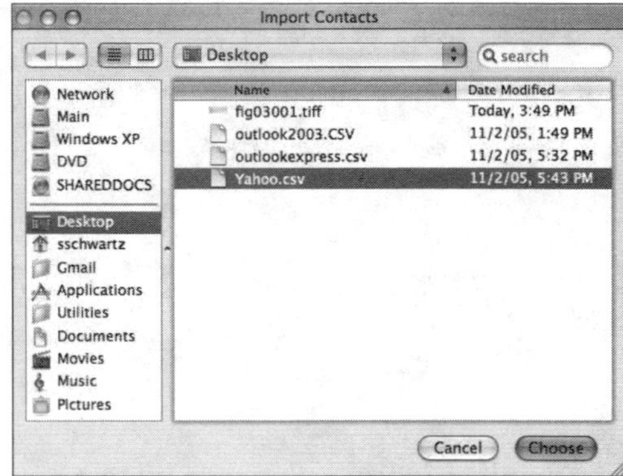

Figure 3.10 Navigate to the folder in which the CSV file is stored, select the file, and then click Choose (or Open).

✔ Tips

- If you have a spreadsheet program, you can use it to check your export file before importing its data into Gmail. You can make any necessary edits in the worksheet, such as deleting unwanted contacts.
- When importing, Gmail checks for duplicates by examining each email address. If the address already exists in Contacts, the old record is replaced by the new data.

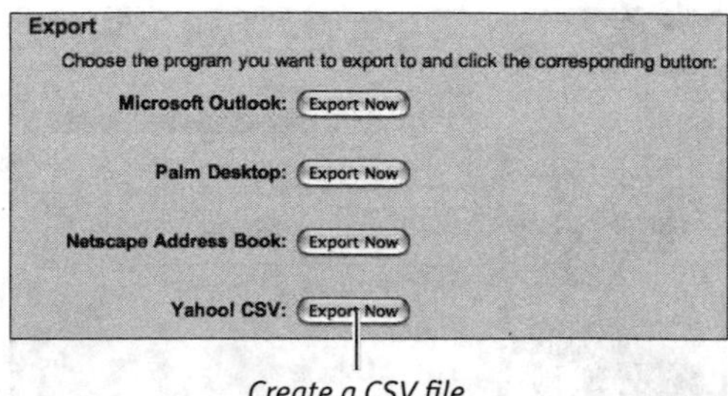

Figure 3.11 Click this button to create a CSV file from your Yahoo! Address Book.

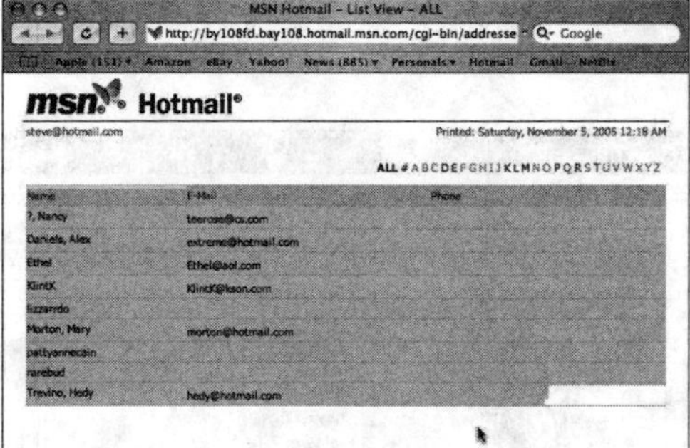

Figure 3.12 If your browser allows it, you can highlight and copy your Hotmail contact data.

To export contacts from Yahoo! Mail:

1. Log into your Yahoo! Mail account at *http://mail.yahoo.com.*
2. Click the Addresses tab at the top of the page.

   The Address Book appears.
3. Click the Import/Export link.
4. In the Export section of the new page (**Figure 3.11**), click the Export Now button beside Yahoo! CSV.

   A file named Yahoo.csv is saved in your browser's default download location. Follow the steps on page 24 to import the data into Gmail.

✔ Tip

- If you use Yahoo! Messenger, contact records will be exported for your chat buddies, too—even if some don't include an email address. Since you can email a buddy at *chatname*@yahoo.com, you can create an email address for each one by editing her or his record in Gmail.

To copy contacts from MSN Hotmail:

1. Use your Web browser to log into your Hotmail account at *www.hotmail.com.*
2. Click the Contacts tab.
3. On the new page, click the Print View link.

   Your contacts appear in a new window.
4. Click to the left of the Name heading, drag down to select all the contact data (**Figure 3.12**), and choose Edit > Copy.
5. Launch Excel or another spreadsheet program, select cell A1, and choose Edit > Paste.
6. If necessary, edit the contact data. Then save it as a CSV file. Follow the steps on page 24 to import the data into Gmail.

To export contacts from Microsoft Office Outlook 2003 (Windows):

1. In Outlook 2003, choose File > Import and Export.

   The Import and Export Wizard appears (**Figure 3.13**).

2. Select Export to a file and click Next.

3. On the Export to a File screen, select Comma Separated Values (Windows) and click Next.

4. On the next screen (**Figure 3.14**), select Contacts as the data to be exported. Click Next.

5. On the next screen, click Browse and then select a location for the export file. Click Next.

6. On the final screen, click Finish.

   The export file (contacts.csv) is created and saved in the specified location. Follow the steps on page 24 to import the data into Gmail.

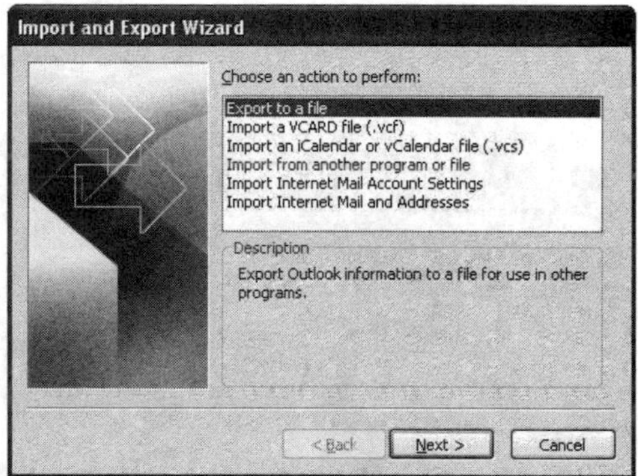

Figure 3.13 Use the Import and Export Wizard to create a CSV file from your Outlook contacts.

Figure 3.14 Select Contacts as the data to be exported.

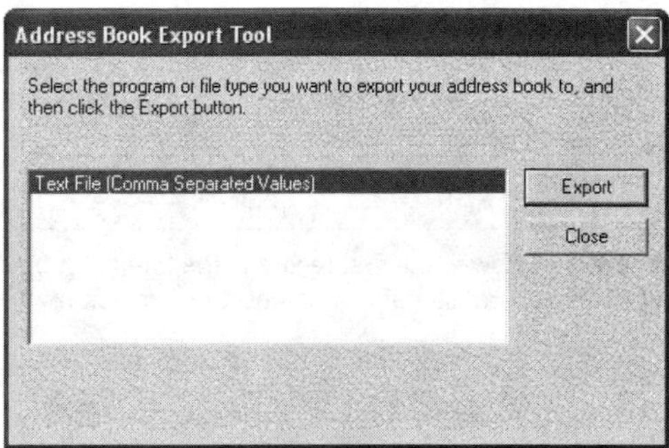

Figure 3.15 Outlook Express provides a wizard that walks you through the process of creating a contacts CSV file.

To export contacts from Microsoft Outlook Express 6 (Windows):

1. In Outlook Express, choose File > Export > Address Book.

   The Address Book Export Tool appears (**Figure 3.15**).

2. Select Text File (Comma Separated Values) and click Export.

3. In the CSV Export dialog box, click Browse.

4. In the Save As dialog box that appears, select a location for the export file, enter a name for it in the File name box, and click Save.

   The CSV Export dialog box reappears.

5. Click Next and then click Finish.

   Follow the steps on page 24 to import the data into Gmail.

To export contacts from another program:

1. In your email program, find the command to export your contacts to a new file.

   Look for an Export or Save As command.

2. If it's an option, save the contact data as a CSV file. If CSV isn't a supported file format, save as a tab-delimited text file.

3. Open the export file in a spreadsheet program. Most can read both CSV and tab-delimited files.

4. Make any necessary edits to the data.

   Ensure that every cell in row 1 contains a heading (**Figure 3.16**) that describes the column's contents, such as Name, Email, or Street Address. (If there is no header row, you must create one with appropriate labels.)

5. Save the file in CSV format. Then import the new file into Gmail.

✔ Tips

- When examining the exported data in a worksheet, each row corresponds to a single contact record. Ensure that no record/row contains excessive data. (Gmail rejects extremely large records.) If so, edit the record by eliminating unnecessary data or by deleting unimportant columns.

- Email programs aren't the only repositories of contact data. You may have a database or utility in which you store such data, for example. Review the program's documentation to see if it can export to a comma-separated or tab-delimited file.

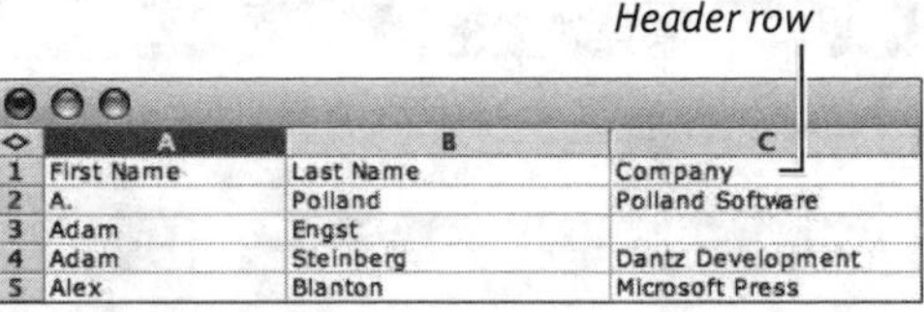

Figure 3.16 Row 1 (the first record in the file) must be a header record, containing names for the columns of data.

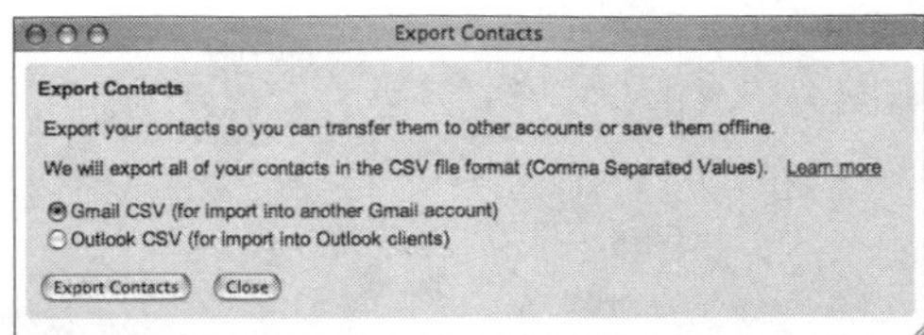

Figure 3.17 Select a CSV output format and click Export Contacts.

Exporting Gmail Contacts

In addition to being able to import contact files, Gmail can also *export* contacts to a CSV file. If you decide to switch email programs, you can use the Export procedure to create a file that the new program can read.

To export your Contacts data:

1. Click the Contacts link on the left side of any Gmail page.
2. Click the Export link on right side of the Contacts page.

   The Export Contacts window opens (**Figure 3.17**).
3. *Do one of the following:*
   - ▲ If you intend to transfer or copy your contacts to another Gmail account, select Gmail CSV as the output format.
   - ▲ To transfer or copy your contacts to Microsoft Office Outlook or Microsoft Outlook Express, select Outlook CSV.
   - ▲ To transfer data to a different program, try both output formats.
4. Click the Export Contacts button.

   The file (gmail.csv or gmail-to-outlook.csv) is created and saved in your browser's default download location. See the new email program's documentation for instructions on importing this contact file.

✔ Tips

- If your email program cannot import a CSV file, open the file in Excel or another spreadsheet program and save the file in a compatible format.
- Even if you don't intend to transfer your Gmail contacts to another program, it's a good idea to periodically run the Export procedure. The resulting file will serve as a *backup* of your contact data.

4

Receiving and Reading Mail

If you use Gmail to send messages to friends, relatives, coworkers, and Internet vendors, you're sure to receive a lot of email. In this chapter, you'll learn to do the following with incoming mail:

- Check for new mail
- Read messages and conversations
- View and save attachments
- Use Gmail Notifier or Google Talk to check for new messages when Gmail isn't open in a browser
- Use an Atom news aggregator to check for new Gmail messages
- Print messages and conversations

To learn how to reply to and forward messages, see Chapter 5. For information about managing your mail (such as adding stars, applying labels, and archiving messages), see Chapter 6.

Checking for New Mail

To check for new incoming mail in other email applications, you click Send/Receive (or choose an equivalent command) or you create an automated schedule. Gmail simplifies the process.

To check for new mail:

- **Gmail, standard version.** The Java program automatically checks for and displays new email every two minutes.

  As long as a Gmail page is displayed in your browser, Gmail will continue to check for new mail.

- **Gmail, basic version.** No automatic checking for new mail occurs. The following actions force a check for new email:
  - Using your browser to view your Gmail account.
  - Refreshing the current Gmail page or performing any action that results in a page refresh.

✔ Tips

- You can cause a page refresh in either the basic or standard version of Gmail by clicking the Refresh link on any Gmail page (**Figure 4.1**), issuing your browser's Refresh or Reload command (**Figure 4.2**), or viewing another Gmail page (such as All Mail or Trash, for example). Performing any of these actions will cause Gmail to check for new messages.
- You can install Gmail Notifier or Google Talk to receive notifications of new email when you don't have the Gmail site open. Gmail Notifier and Google Talk are both discussed later in this chapter.

Figure 4.1 Click Refresh to reload the current Gmail page and to check for new email.

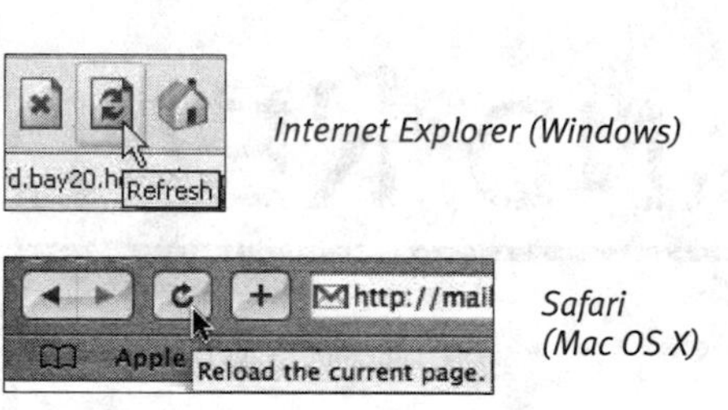

Figure 4.2 Issuing the browser's Refresh or Reload command also causes Gmail to check for new mail.

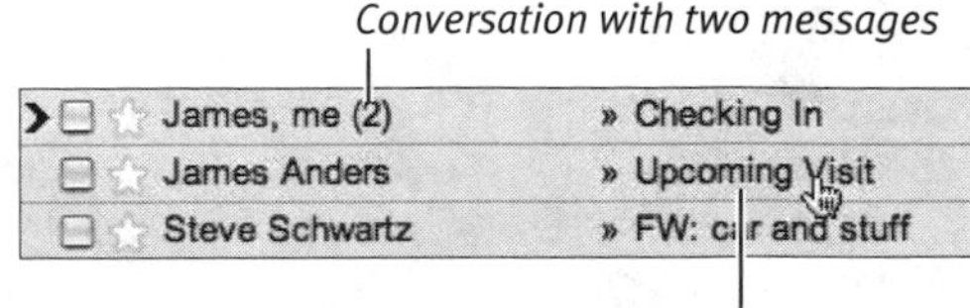

Figure 4.3 Click the header of the message you want to read.

Return to message list

Figure 4.4 The message opens for you to read.

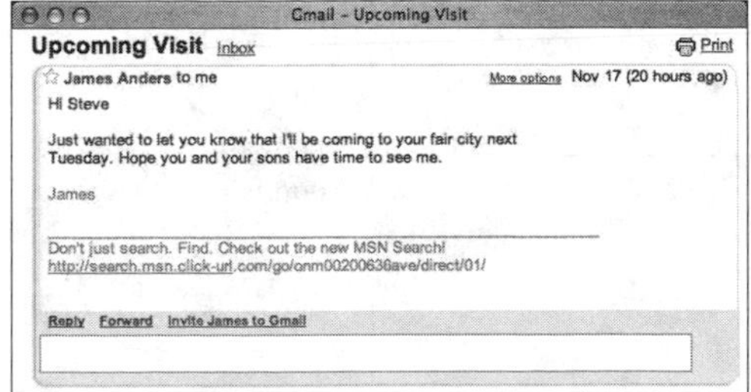

Figure 4.5 If you find it more convenient, you can open any message in a separate window.

Reading Messages and Conversations

Regardless of where it's stored in Gmail, you can read messages you've received or sent. As explained in Chapter 2, sent and received messages with the same Subject are grouped into a Gmail *conversation*. Because reading a conversation is slightly different than reading a lone message, they are explained separately below.

To read a message:

1. Display a Gmail page that lists the message you want to read.

   A single message has no number after the sender or recipient's name. A *conversation* (two or more related messages) is indicated by a number after the participants' names. The number denotes the number of messages in the conversation.

2. Click anywhere in the header of the message you want to read (**Figure 4.3**).

   The message is displayed (**Figure 4.4**).

3. While reading the message, you can also do the following:

   ▲ Click New window to open the message in a separate window (**Figure 4.5**).

   ▲ Click Print to print the message.

   ▲ Click Reply or Forward to reply to the message or forward it to someone else.

   ▲ If the message was selected in the Inbox, click the Archive button to remove it from the Inbox. (A copy will still be available in All Mail.)

   ▲ To report the message as junk mail, click Report Spam.

   ▲ Delete the message by selecting Move to Trash from the More Actions menu.

   ▲ Click More options to reveal other message-handling options.

continues on next page

4. When you're done reading the message, you can do either of the following:
   - ▲ Return to the original message list by clicking the Back to Inbox link (or whatever list you were originally viewing).
   - ▲ Go to a different message list by clicking its link on the left side of the page (**Figure 4.6**).

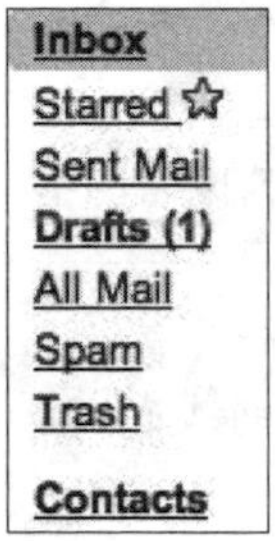

Inbox
Starred ☆
Sent Mail
Drafts (1)
All Mail
Spam
Trash

Contacts

Figure 4.6 Select a Gmail message list by clicking one of these links.

To read a conversation:

1. Display a Gmail page that lists the conversation you want to read.
2. Click anywhere in the conversation's header (see Figure 4.3).

   The conversation is displayed (**Figure 4.7**). The most recent message (at the bottom of the message stack) is shown. The other messages are collapsed.

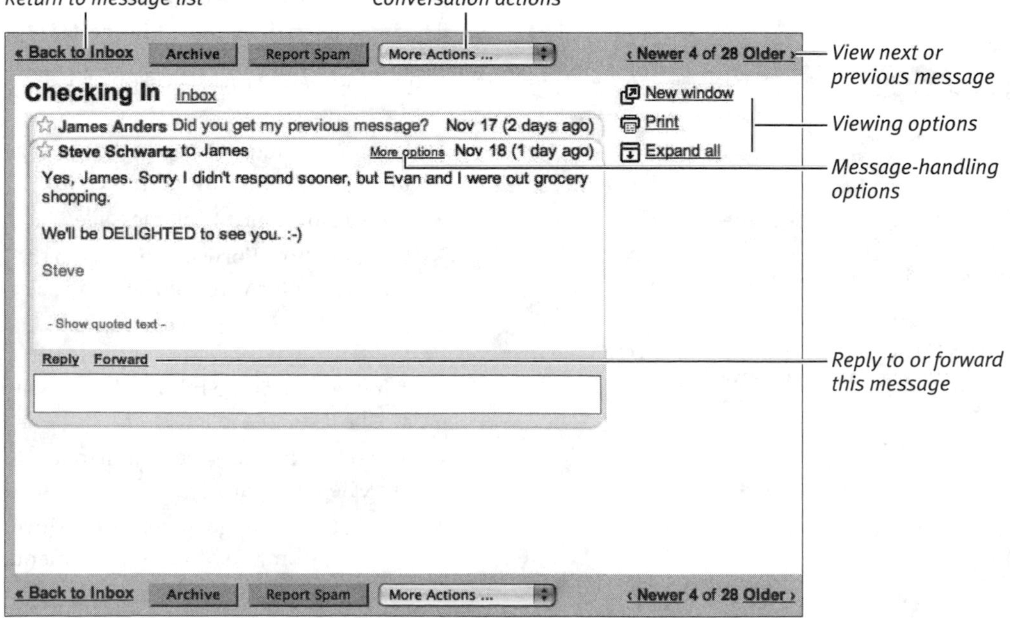

Figure 4.7 All messages in a conversation are displayed in a stack. The oldest message is on the top and the newest is on the bottom.

Figure 4.8 Choose an action to apply to the conversation from the More Actions menu.

3. *Do any of the following:*
   - ▲ Click New Window to read the conversation in a separate window.
   - ▲ To expand a message in the conversation, click its header. To collapse the message, click its header again.
   - ▲ Click Expand all to expand all messages in the conversation. To reverse this action, click Collapse all.
   - ▲ To apply an action to the entire conversation, such as marking it with a star or moving it to the Trash, choose a More Actions option (**Figure 4.8**). (See Chapter 6 for more information.)
   - ▲ You can add or remove the star from any message in the conversation by clicking the message's star.
   - ▲ Click the Archive button to remove the conversation from the Inbox. (You can still read an archived conversation in All Mail, as well as in any labels that you've applied to the conversation.)
   - ▲ To write a reply to or forward a message in the conversation, click the Reply or Forward link beneath the message.
   - ▲ To print all messages in the conversation, click the Print link. (For detailed information about printing messages, see "Printing Messages," later in this chapter.)
4. *Do one of the following:*
   - ▲ To read other messages (in order), click the Newer or Older link.
   - ▲ To return to the original Gmail page, click Back to *list* (found above and below the conversation).
   - ▲ To go to a different Gmail section, click its link on the left side of the page (see Figure 4.6).

✔ Tip

- ■ The most recent message in a conversation—the one on the bottom—cannot be collapsed. It is always displayed.

Working with Attachments

Gmail can send or receive messages with one or multiple *attachments* (attached files). The total size of the attachments, however, cannot exceed 10 MB after Gmail encodes the file(s) for mailing.

A message with one or more attachments is marked with a paper clip icon. The icon is displayed in the message header in message lists and to the right of the sender's name when reading the message (**Figure 4.9**).

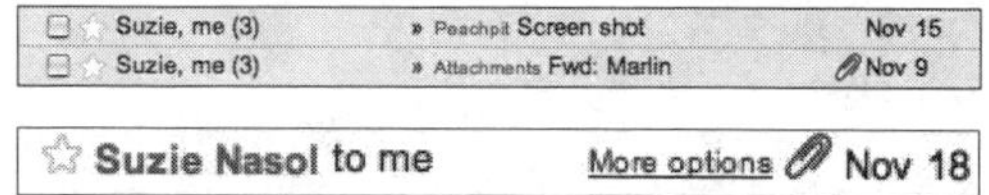

Figure 4.9 Attachments are indicated by a paper clip in a message list (top) or an open message (bottom).

To open or view file attachments:

- *Do any of the following:*
  - Certain types of image attachments, such as JPEG and GIF files, are displayed in the message (**Figure 4.10**).
  - To view compatible images in a new browser window, click View or View All Images. (Images shown in a message are often reduced in size. Clicking a View link displays them at full size.)
  - To download a single attachment, click the Download link beside the filename or file icon (see Figure 4.10).
  - When you want to save all attachments to a message, click Download all attachments. Gmail creates a Zip archive, compresses all of the attachments, and then downloads them to your computer.

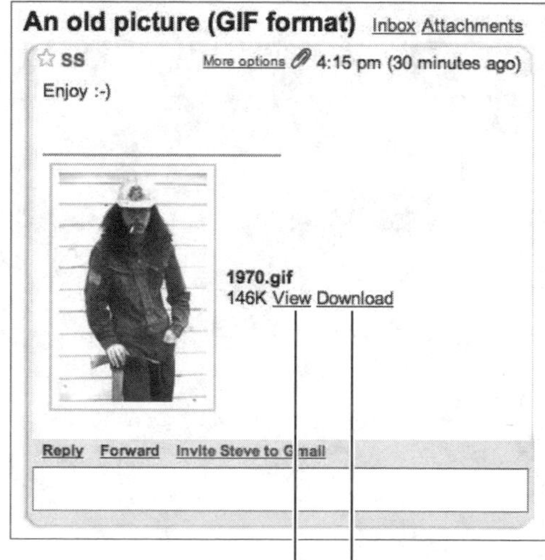

Figure 4.10 Some types of image attachments can be displayed within the message.

✔ Tips

- If someone sends you a large attachment that never arrives, it probably exceeded the 10 MB limit. Suggest that the sender split the attachments among multiple messages or use a utility to compress the files, such as WinZip (Windows) or StuffIt (Mac).
- When downloading multiple attachments as a zip archive, you'll need a utility to extract the files from the archive. Two of the most popular are:
  - **Windows:** WinZip (*www.winzip.com*)
  - **Mac:** StuffIt (*www.allume.com*)

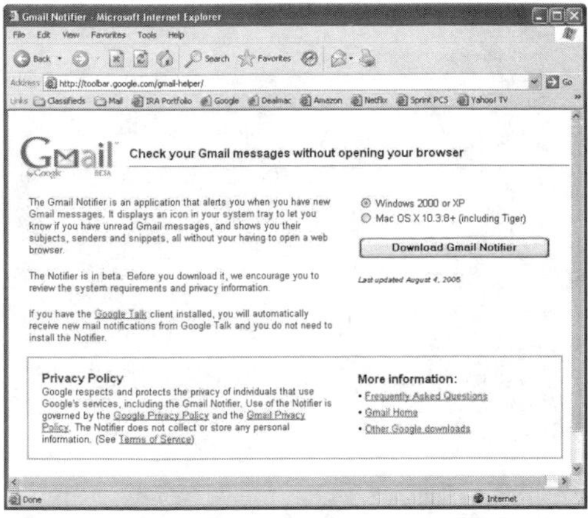

Figure 4.11 Download Gmail Notifier from this page.

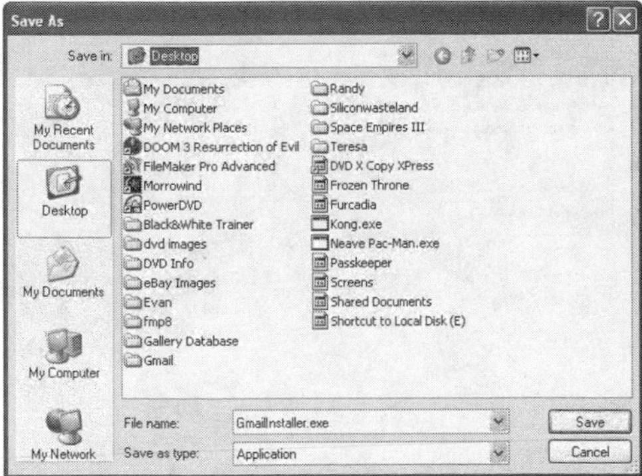

Figure 4.12 Select a drive and folder in which to store the installation program.

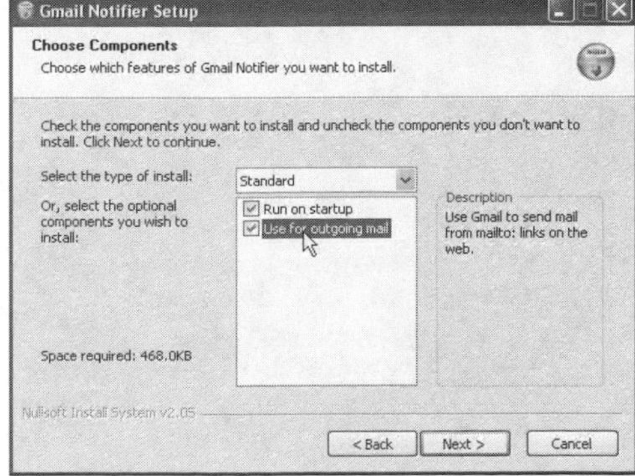

Figure 4.13 Select installation options and click Next.

Using Gmail Notifier

Even if you use Gmail as a primary email account, you may not want to keep a browser window open just to check for new mail. If you still want to be notified quickly when email arrives, you can install Gmail Notifier, a free Google application for Windows and Mac OS X.

To install Gmail Notifier (Windows):

1. In Gmail, click the Settings link. Near the bottom of the General settings tab, click Get the Gmail Notifier.
2. On the new Web page, click the Windows 2000 or XP radio button, and then click Download Gmail Notifier (**Figure 4.11**).

   A File Download dialog box appears.
3. Click the Save button.
4. In the Save As dialog box (**Figure 4.12**), select a convenient location in which to save the installation program, such as the Desktop. Then click Save.
5. After the file (GmailInstaller.exe) downloads to your computer, click its file icon to launch the installation program. Click Run in the Open File dialog box.
6. In the Gmail Notifier Setup dialog box, click I Agree to accept the license agreement.
7. On the Choose Components screen (**Figure 4.13**), select Standard install. Click the check boxes of desired options, and click Next.
   - Select Run on startup to automatically run the program each time you start Windows.
   - Select Use for outgoing mail to make Gmail the default email client to use when you click a *mailto:* link on a Web page.

continues on next page

8. On the Choose Install Location screen, select the folder on your hard disk in which to install the program. Click Next to continue.

   To select a drive and folder other than the proposed one, click Browse.

9. On the Choose Start Menu Folder screen (**Figure 4.14**), specify the Windows Start Menu folder in which the application will be stored and listed. Click Install to continue.

   ▲ To create a new main level Start folder, accept the default folder name (Gmail Notifier).

   ▲ To store the application in an existing Start Menu folder, select the folder from the list.

   Gmail Notifier is installed on your PC.

10. Click Close to dismiss the final dialog box (**Figure 4.15**).

    Optionally, you can view the installation details by clicking Show details.

To launch Gmail Notifier (Windows):

◆ *Do one of the following:*

  ▲ During installation, if you selected the option to Run on startup (see Step 7 of the previous step list), Gmail automatically launches at the start of each computing session.

  ▲ Click the Start > All Programs, and choose Gmail Notifier from the Start Menu folder in which it was installed.

  Gmail Notifier launches and its icon appears in the system tray (at the right end of the Windows taskbar).

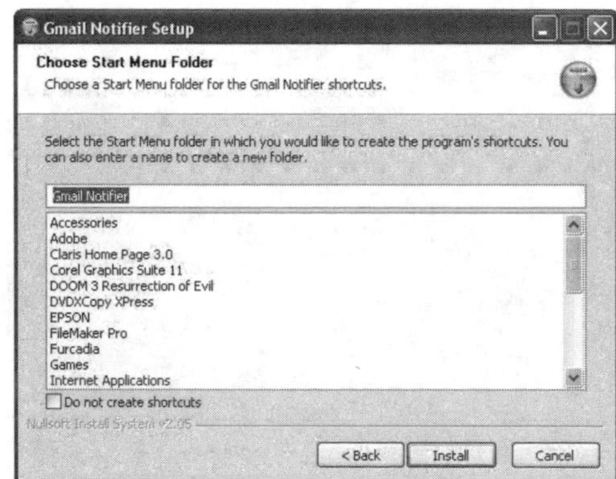

Figure 4.14 Create a Start Menu folder for Gmail Notifier or pick an existing folder in which to store it.

Review the details of the installation

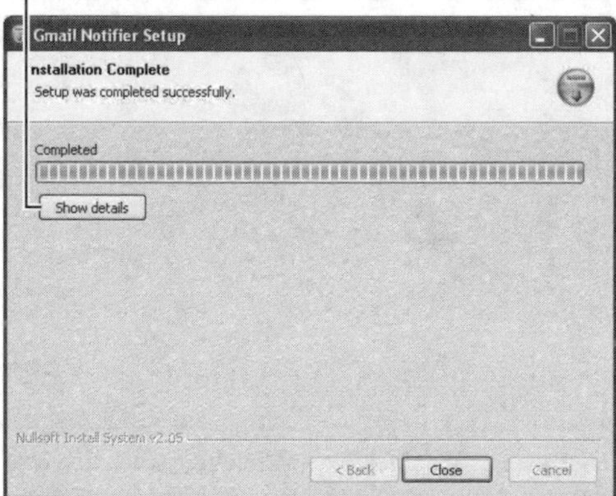

Figure 4.15 To review the installation details, click Show details. When you're finished, click Close.

USING GMAIL NOTIFIER

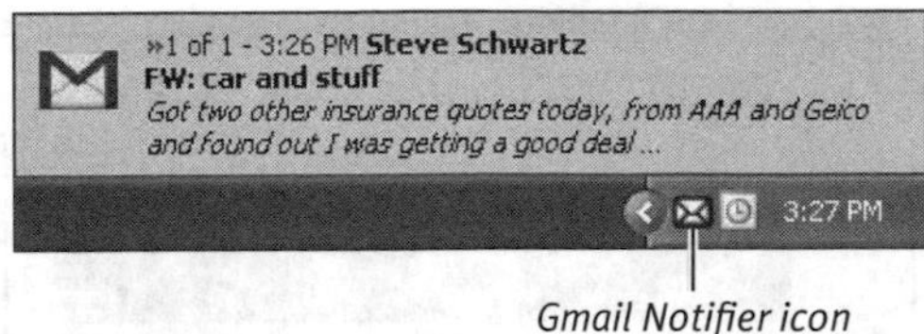

Figure 4.16 When new mail is detected, Notifier opens this small window above the system tray.

Figure 4.17 Right-click the Notifier icon to display this pop-up menu.

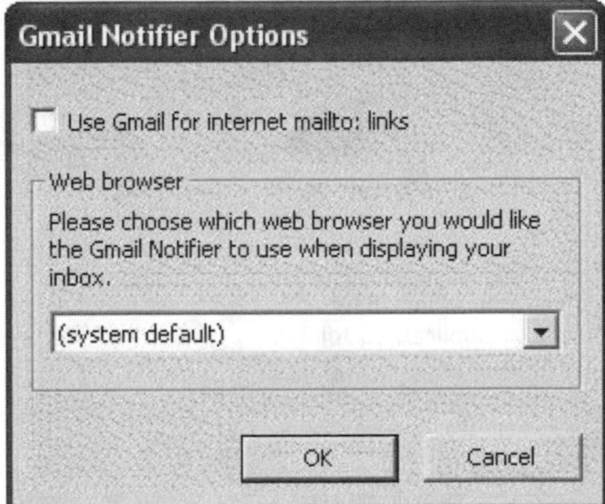

Figure 4.18 You can change Notifier settings in this dialog box.

To use Gmail Notifier (Windows):

- *Do any of the following:*
  - When a new message arrives, Notifier opens a small window containing a snippet of the message (**Figure 4.16**). To read the message, double-click the Notifier icon, or right-click the icon and choose View Inbox from the pop-up menu that appears (**Figure 4.17**).

    Your browser launches and displays your Gmail Inbox.
  - After displaying the message snippet for a few seconds, the tiny window disappears. To see the snippet again, right-click the Notifier icon and choose Tell Me Again.
  - To instruct Notifier to immediately check for new messages, right-click the Notifier icon and choose Check Mail Now.
  - To shut down Notifier, right-click the Notifier icon and choose Exit.

To set Gmail Notifier preferences (Windows):

1. Right-click the Notifier icon and choose Options from the pop-up menu.

   The Gmail Notifier Options dialog box appears (**Figure 4.18**).
2. If you want Gmail to be treated as your default email program, click the Use Gmail for Internet mailto: links.

   When you click an email link on a Web page, your browser will launch and take you to the Gmail site.
3. To specify a particular Web browser to use when Notifier is asked to display your Gmail Inbox, select it from the drop-down list.
4. Click OK to close the dialog box and save the new settings. Or click Cancel to ignore any changes you've made.

To uninstall Gmail Notifier (Windows):

1. Open the Add or Remove Programs control panel.

   If you're running Windows XP, click the Start button, choose Control Panel, and click the Add or Remove Programs icon.

2. In the Add or Remove Programs window (**Figure 4.19**), select Google Gmail Notifier.

3. To uninstall Gmail Notifier, click the Remove button.

   The Gmail Notifier Uninstall dialog box appears.

4. Click the Uninstall button.

   Gmail Notifier is removed from your computer.

5. Click Close to dismiss the dialog box.

   Optionally, you can click Show Details to review the specific items that were removed.

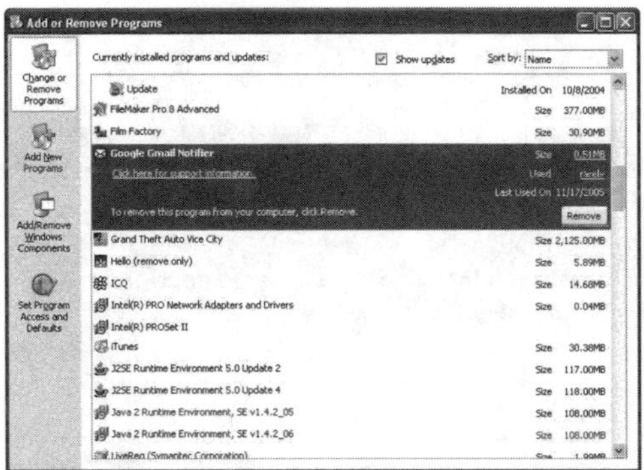

Figure 4.19 Select Google Gmail Notifier and click Remove.

✔ Tip

- Even if you miss a new message notification, the lines in the Notifier icon turn dark blue to indicate that there are unread messages. When you move the cursor over the icon, it shows the number of unread messages awaiting you.

Figure 4.20 To install Gmail Notifier, drag this icon into your Applications folder.

To install Gmail Notifier (Mac OS X):

1. In Gmail, click the Settings link. Near the bottom of the General settings tab, click Get the Gmail Notifier.

2. On the new Web page, click the Mac OS X radio button, and click Download Gmail Notifier (see Figure 4.11).

   The application downloads and the installation screen appears (**Figure 4.20**).

3. Drag the Gmail Notifier icon into your Applications folder.

4. Close the dialog box.

✔ Tips

- When installing Gmail Notifier for Mac OS X, double-click the downloaded file if the installation screen doesn't appear.
- After successfully installing Gmail Notifier, you can drag the Gmail Notifier and GmailNotifier.dmg icons into the Trash.

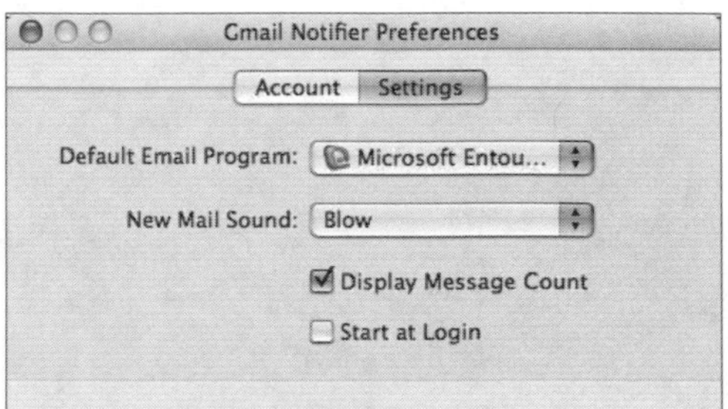

Figure 4.21 You can instruct Gmail Notifier to automatically run every time you turn on your Mac.

Figure 4.22 When it is active, the Gmail Notifier icon appears in the menu bar.

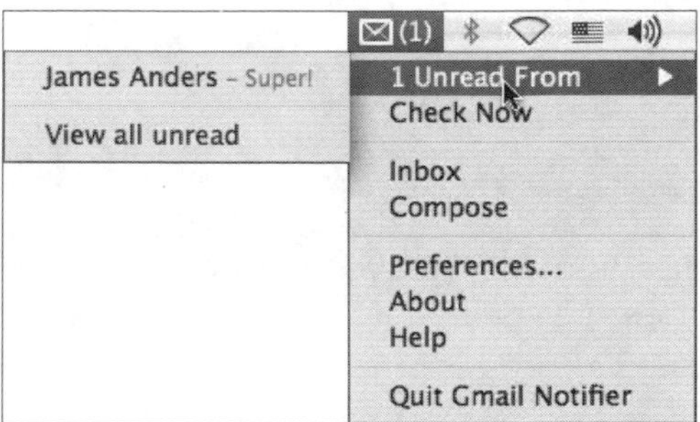

Figure 4.23 Click the Gmail Notifier icon to reveal this pop-up menu.

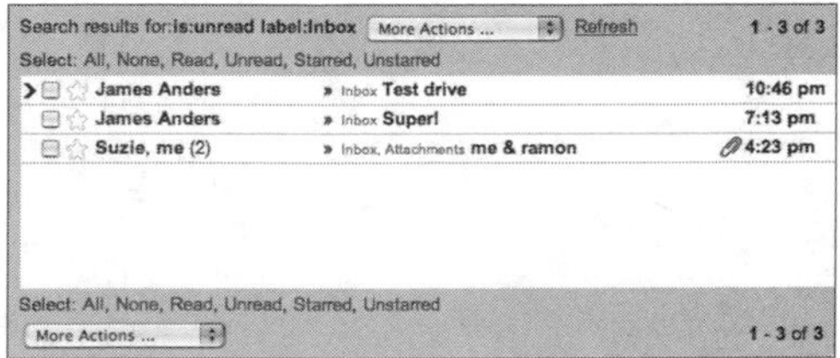

Figure 4.24 Choosing the View all unread command causes Gmail to execute a search for all unread email in the Inbox.

To launch Gmail Notifier (Mac OS X):

- *Do one of the following:*
  - Double-click the Gmail Notifier icon in the Applications folder.
  - Set Gmail Notifier to automatically launch at startup.

    Click the Notifier icon in the menu bar and choose Preferences from the pop-up menu. Click the Settings tab in the Gmail Notifier Preferences dialog box (**Figure 4.21**), click the Start at Login check box, and close the dialog box.

  Gmail Notifier's icon appears in the menu bar (**Figure 4.22**).

To use Gmail Notifier (Mac OS X):

- *Do any of the following:*
  - When new messages arrive, the Notifier icon turns bright blue. To read a message, click the Notifier icon and choose the unread message (**Figure 4.23**). The message opens in your browser.
  - To go to your Gmail Inbox, choose Inbox from the pop-up menu.
  - To display all unread messages in a new Gmail window (**Figure 4.24**), choose View all unread from the pop-up menu.
  - To instruct Notifier to immediately check for new messages, choose Check Now from the pop-up menu.
  - To create a new message, choose Compose from the pop-up menu.
  - Choose Help from the pop-up menu to open Gmail Help in your browser.
  - To shut down Notifier, choose Quit Gmail Notifier from the pop-up menu.

To set Gmail Notifier preferences (Mac OS X):

1. Choose Preferences from the pop-up menu.

   The Gmail Notifier Preferences dialog box appears.

2. On the Accounts tab (**Figure 4.25**), enter your Gmail user name and password. To instruct Mac OS X to remember and automatically use your password, click Save Password in Keychain.

3. On the Settings tab (see Figure 4.21), you can set these preferences:
   - ▲ Select a Default Email Program from the pop-up list. If you select Gmail, when you click an email link on a Web page, your browser will launch and take you to the Gmail site.
   - ▲ From the New Mail Sound pop-up list, select a sound effect for Notifier to use to announce new Gmail messages.
   - ▲ To display the number of new messages beside the Gmail Notifier icon, click the Display Message Count check box.
   - ▲ To make Gmail Notifier automatically launch each time you start a computing session, click Start at Login.

4. Close the Gmail Notifier Preferences dialog box.

   The new settings are saved.

To uninstall Gmail Notifier (Mac OS X):

1. Open your Applications folder, and drag the Gmail Notifier file into the Trash.

2. Delete the com.google.GmailNotifier.plist preferences file. (This file can be found in the Preferences folder within your user folder.)

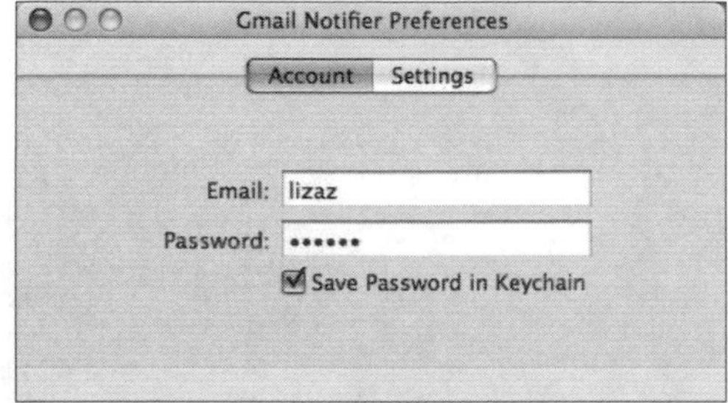

Figure 4.25 Enter your Gmail account information on the Account tab of the Preferences dialog box.

Figure 4.26 Enter the Gmail address in the aggregator's URL or Address box.

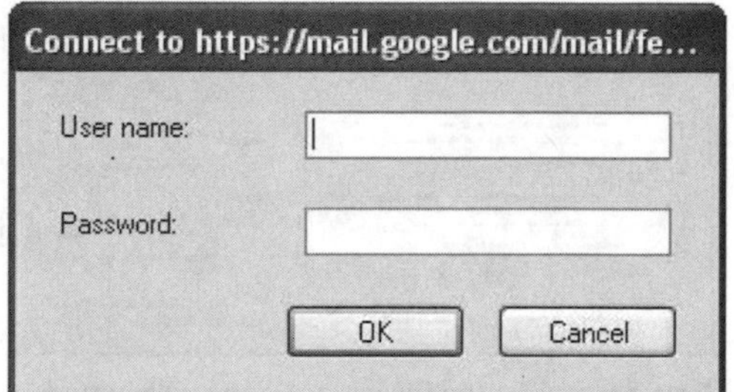

Figure 4.27 Enter your Gmail user name and password.

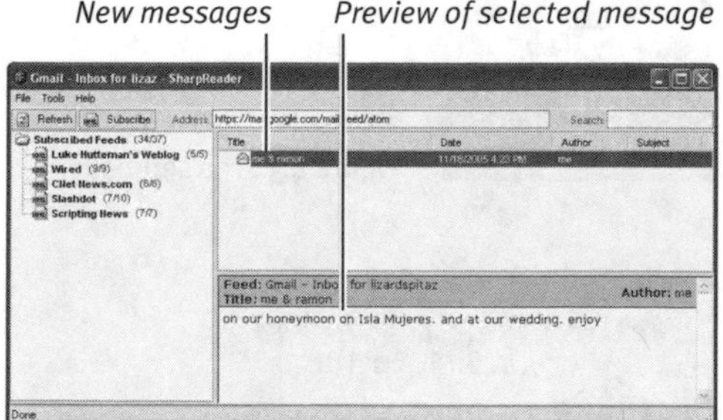

Figure 4.28 A preview of the selected Gmail message is displayed.

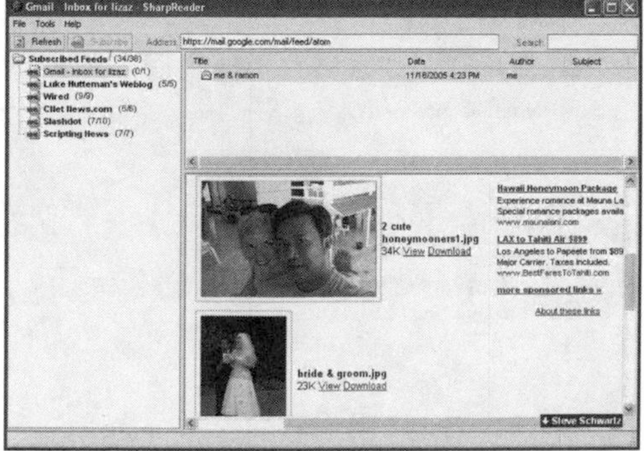

Figure 4.29 SharpReader's preview pane also acts as a browser.

New Mail Notification via Atom Feed

If you employ a newsreader/aggregator to keep up with the latest news and blog postings, you can also use it to receive instant notification of new Gmail messages.

Note that the aggregator must support Atom 0.3, SSL/HTTPS, and HTTP authentication. In the example below, I'm using SharpReader (*http://www.sharpreader.net*) as my Windows news aggregator.

To configure an aggregator to receive Gmail data:

1. Launch the aggregator.
2. Enter the following in the Address box or URL field (**Figure 4.26**):

   https://gmail.google.com/gmail/feed/atom
3. When prompted (**Figure 4.27**), enter your Gmail user name and password. Click OK.

   New messages in your Inbox (if any) are displayed (**Figure 4.28**).
4. To subscribe to the Gmail feed, click the Subscribe button.
5. Double-click any message to view your Inbox in the preview pane.

   SharpReader's preview pane doubles as a Web browser. You can now use normal Gmail procedures to read messages of interest (**Figure 4.29**).

✔ Tip

- Google suggests that you configure your aggregator to check for new mail every 10 minutes or so. To configure SharpReader, right-click the Gmail subscription (in the left pane) and choose Properties. In the Feed pane that appears, set RefreshRate to Every 15 Minutes.

New Mail Notification via Google Talk

Another way to receive instant notification of new Gmail messages is to install and run Google Talk, a free text and voice chat program from Google.

To install Google Talk (Windows):

1. In Gmail, click the Settings link. Near the bottom of the General settings tab, click Get Google Talk.
2. On the new Web page (**Figure 4.30**), click the Download Google Talk button.
3. In the File Download dialog box that appears, click the Save button.
   A Save As dialog box appears.
4. Select an easy-to-find location (such as the Desktop) in which to save the setup program, and click Save.
   The file googletalk-setup.exe downloads to your computer (**Figure 4.31**).
5. Click the icon of the downloaded file.
   The setup program launches and an Open File dialog box appears.
6. Click the Run button.
7. In the License Agreement dialog box, click I Agree.
   The program is installed and the Google Talk window appears (**Figure 4.32**).
8. Enter your Gmail user name and password, and click Sign In.
   Google Talk logs you in.

✔ Tip

- After you've installed Google Talk, you can throw away the googletalk-setup.exe file. If you later need to reinstall Google Talk, you can download the latest version.

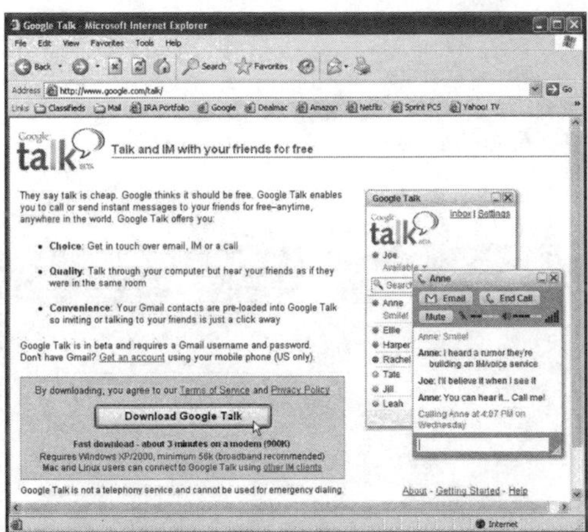

Figure 4.30 Click the Download Google Talk button.

Figure 4.31 The setup file.

Figure 4.32 Sign in to Google Talk by entering your Gmail user name and password.

Figure 4.33 This icon is added to the Desktop during installation.

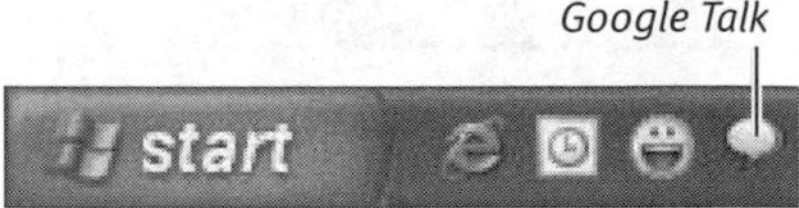

Figure 4.34 If you drag the Google Talk icon onto the Quick Launch bar (to the right of the Start button), you can launch it from there.

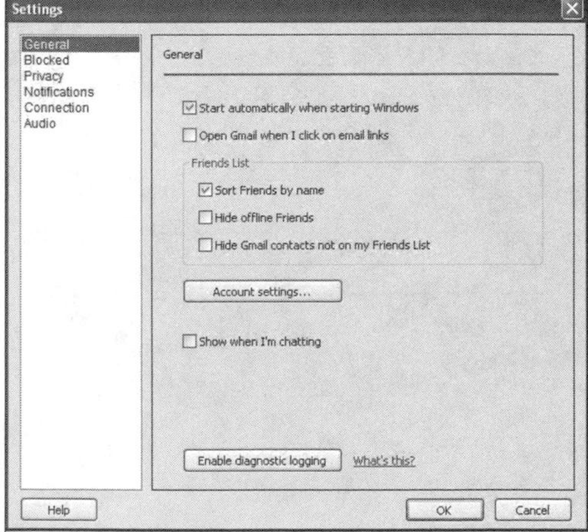

Figure 4.35 The Start automatically when starting Windows setting determines whether Google Talk launches at the start of each computing session.

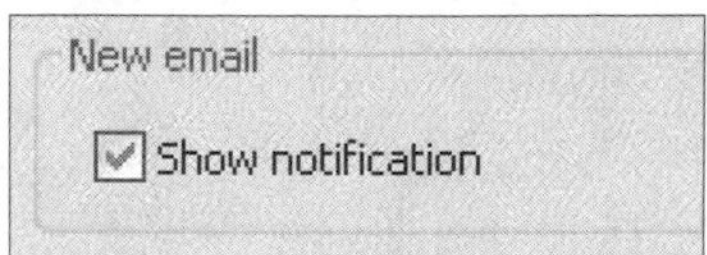

Figure 4.36 This setting governs whether you receive notifications of new Gmail messages.

To launch Google Talk:

- *Do one of the following:*
  - Click the Google Talk icon that was placed on the Desktop during the installation (**Figure 4.33**).
  - Click the Windows Start button and move the cursor over All Programs. Choose Google Talk from the Google Talk folder in the Start Menu.

✔ Tips

- If you're using Windows XP, you can drag the Google Talk icon from the Desktop onto the Quick Launch bar. Then to launch Google Talk, all you'll have to do is click its Quick Launch icon (**Figure 4.34**).
- If you add Google Talk to the Quick Launch bar, you can delete the Desktop icon.

To configure Google Talk:

1. Launch Google Talk by clicking its icon on the Desktop or by choosing its name from the Start > All Programs menu.
2. Click the Settings text at the top of the Google Talk window (see Figure 4.32).

   The Settings dialog box appears.
3. *Optional:* In the General section (**Figure 4.35**), remove the check mark from Start automatically when starting Windows. If you disable this option, you can still manually launch Google Talk as needed.
4. Click the Notifications text in the left pane. The Show notification option for New email (**Figure 4.36**) determines whether you receive instant notifications of new Gmail messages. Ensure that this option is checked.
5. Click OK to save your settings changes.

To handle new message notifications:

1. When Google Talk notices that your Gmail account has received new messages, a notification window appears above the system tray (**Figure 4.37**).
2. *Do any of the following:*
   - ▲ If there are multiple new messages, click the arrow icons to review the different messages.
   - ▲ If there's a message you want to read, move the cursor over the M icon. When the M turns red, click it to view the new message in your browser.
   - ▲ To go to your Inbox rather than opening a specific new message, right-click the Google Talk icon in the system tray. Choose Inbox from the pop-up menu that appears (**Figure 4.38**).
   - ▲ Do nothing. In a few seconds, the notification window will disappear.

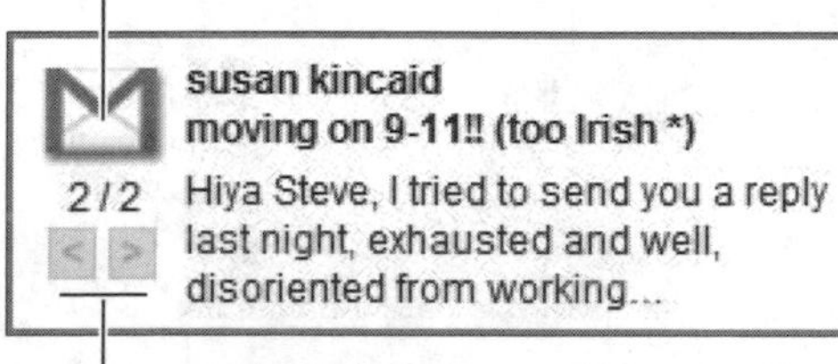

Figure 4.37 New messages are announced in this tiny window. After a few seconds, the window disappears.

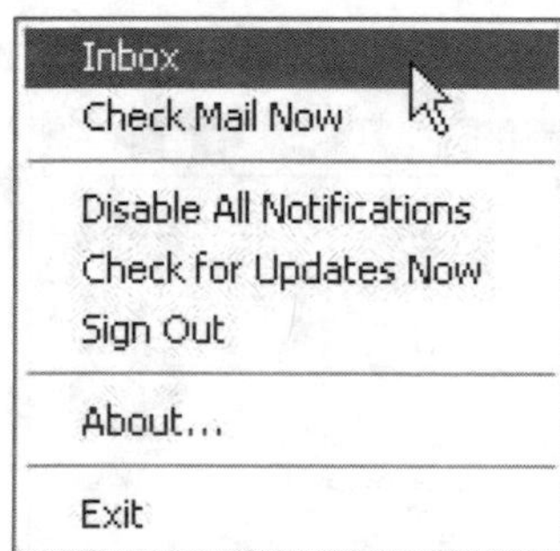

Figure 4.38 Right-click the Google Talk icon in the system tray to reveal this pop-up menu.

To quit/shut down Google Talk:

- ◆ Right-click the Google Talk icon in the system tray and choose Exit from the pop-up menu (see Figure 4.38).

✔ Tip

- ■ You can also use the Google Talk pop-up menu (see Figure 4.38) to immediately check for new email (Check Mail Now), turn off Gmail notifications (Disable All Notifications), or sign out of your account but leave Gmail running (Sign Out).

Google Talk and Mac OS X

While there is no Google Talk client specifically designed for Mac OS X, you can configure iChat as a Jabber client for Gmail by following the instructions at:

http://www.google.com/support/talk/bin/answer.py?answer=24076

Note, however, that only the Windows Google Talk client checks for and notifies you of new Gmail messages.

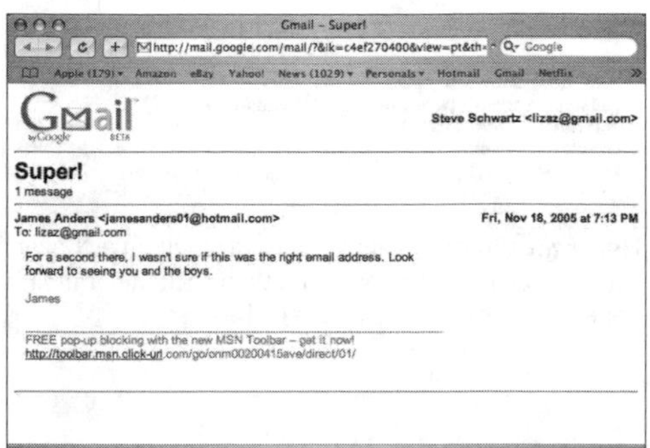

Figure 4.39 Gmail formats the message for printing and displays it in a new window.

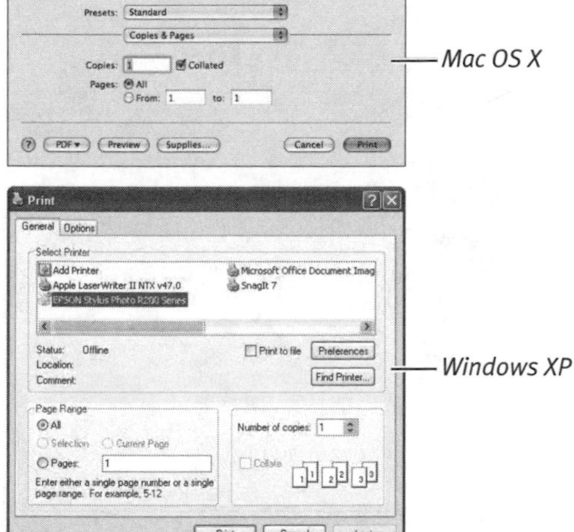

Figure 4.40 Mac OS X and Windows XP Print dialog boxes.

Printing Messages

If you want a printed copy of a message or conversation, Gmail is happy to oblige. When you click the Print link, the selected material appears in a new window, formatted and ready to print. The procedure for printing a single message is slightly different from printing an entire conversation.

To print a single message:

1. Open the message and click the Print link (above and to the right of the message text).

   The formatted message appears in a new browser window (**Figure 4.39**).
2. In the Print dialog box that also appears (**Figure 4.40**), select your printer, set print options, and click Print.
3. Close the new browser window.

To print a conversation:

1. Open the conversation.
2. *Optional:* Quoted text (normally hidden when reading a conversation) can be printed for all messages in the conversation or none. To print all quoted text, click Show quoted text at the bottom of any message in the conversation.
3. Click the Print link (above and to the right of the conversation text).

   The formatted messages appear in a new browser window. All messages are automatically expanded.
4. In the Print dialog box that also appears (see Figure 4.40), select your printer, set print options, and click Print.
5. Close the new browser window.

To print a single message from a conversation:

1. Open the conversation for reading.
2. Expand the message that you want to print by clicking its header.
3. *Optional:* To print quoted text (if any), click the Show quoted text link at the bottom of the message.

   The quoted text appears at the bottom of the message.
4. Click the More options link (found to the right of the selected message's header).

   The message header expands and additional message-handling options appear beneath the header (**Figure 4.41**).
5. Click the Print link beneath the message header.

   The formatted messages appears in a new browser window.
6. In the Print dialog box that also appears (see Figure 4.40), select your printer, set print options, and click Print.
7. Close the new browser window.

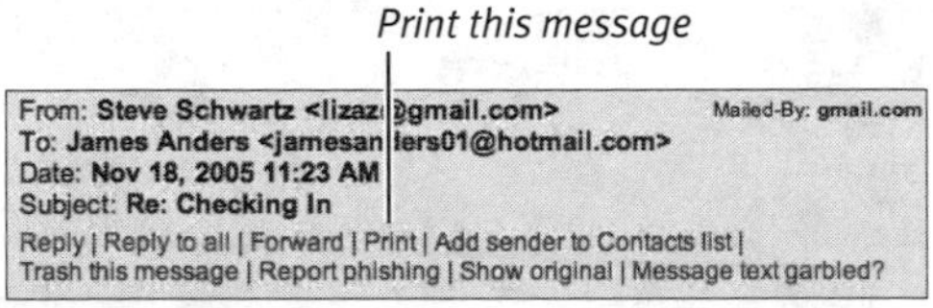

Print this message

From: **Steve Schwartz <lizaz gmail.com>** Mailed-By: **gmail.com**
To: **James Anders <jamesan lers01@hotmail.com>**
Date: **Nov 18, 2005 11:23 AM**
Subject: **Re: Checking In**
Reply | Reply to all | Forward | Print | Add sender to Contacts list |
Trash this message | Report phishing | Show original | Message text garbled?

Figure 4.41 To print a single message within a conversation, click More options, and then click the Print link beneath the expanded message header.

5 Composing and Sending Mail

Email is a two-way thing. Unless all you use Gmail for is reading mailing list messages and advertisements from Internet companies, you'll spend as much time creating, responding to, and forwarding messages as you will reading incoming mail.

In this chapter, you'll learn about:

- Email addresses
- Composing new messages, replying to received messages, and forwarding received messages to others
- Using Gmail's formatting toolbar to create formatted (Rich Text) messages
- Saving unfinished messages as drafts
- Attaching files to your messages
- Using the spell checker to catch typos
- Email etiquette

About Email Addresses

When you send a message, you indicate the intended recipient by specifying his or her email address. Every email address is unique.

An email address (**Figure 5.1**) has two parts: a *user name* and a *domain name* (the service with which the person has an account). The domain might be an Internet service provider (earthlink.net), a company (microsoft.com), an information service (aol.com), or an educational institution (hnrc.tufts.edu).

Every domain name is represented by a suffix (also called a *zone*) that indicates the kind of organization it is. Common suffixes include:

- *.com* (commercial)
- *.net* (network)
- *.org* (organization)
- *.edu* (educational)
- *.gov* (government)

User names are either created by the individual or assigned by his or her service or institution. User names can include letters, numbers, and special characters, such as underscores and periods. Spaces, however, aren't allowed. Although many people on the Internet may have the same user name, there can be only one person with that name in a given domain.

The user and domain name are separated by an @ character. Here are some examples of email addresses:

- `spatterson@aol.com`
  (an America Online address)
- `kandykorn@postoffice.ptd.net`
  (an ISP address)
- `dave73@eng.uchicago.edu`
  (an educational address)

Figure 5.1 Every email address consists of a user name, the @ character, and a domain name.

Gmail Email Addresses

Gmail has two interesting conventions regarding its email addresses. First, you can include periods in your user name to improve readability; Gmail ignores them. For example, bobjones@gmail.com could be entered as *bob.jones@gmail.com.*

Second, you can include a plus (+) after your user name, followed by a text string. When making a purchase from a Web site or registering at one, you could include the site name in the address (for example, *bobjones+ShopNet@gmail.com*). Assuming the retailer or site replies to that address, you can create a *filter* (see Chapter 7) to select those messages. And if the address eventually generates spam, you can modify the filter to send the messages directly to the Trash.

Figure 5.2 A record in Contacts lists a person's name, email address, and other contact information.

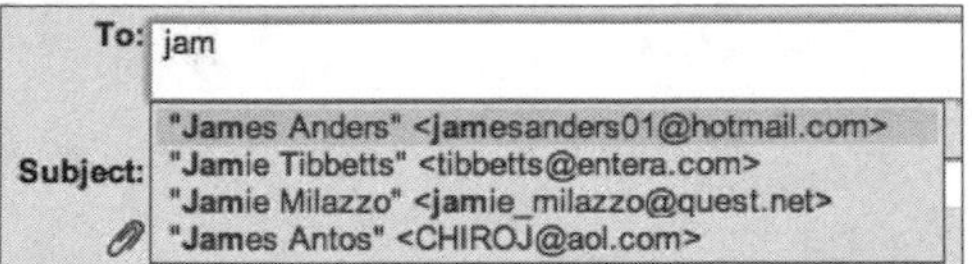

Figure 5.3 When you type a recipient's name, Gmail lists possible matches from your Contacts. People with whom you correspond most are listed first.

As you can see, you may or may not be able to determine a person's name from the email address.

To make it easy to deal with lengthy addresses, email programs usually provide an *address book* or *contacts list* in which to record email addresses (see Chapter 3). In the contacts list, every address is linked to the person's full name, company, and other identifying information (**Figure 5.2**). When addressing messages, you can choose the recipient's name from the contacts list (**Figure 5.3**). Thus, after recording an email address, you'll never have to type it again.

✔ Tips

- Although letter case doesn't matter when addressing email, the convention is to type email addresses entirely in lowercase.
- Whenever you address a message to someone new, Gmail creates a new contact record for that person, company, or institution.
- Gmail's *address autocomplete* (see Figure 5.3) is available in standard view, but not in basic HTML view.

The Message Pane

You can create three types of email messages in Gmail:

- **New messages.** Messages you compose from scratch.
- **Replies.** Responses to received messages.
- **Forwarded messages.** Received messages you are sending to someone else.

All messages are composed in a message pane (**Figure 5.4**). The pane has three sections: the message header (To, Cc, Bcc, and Subject boxes), the attachments list, and the message body (the text of the message). Messages can be formatted or plain text.

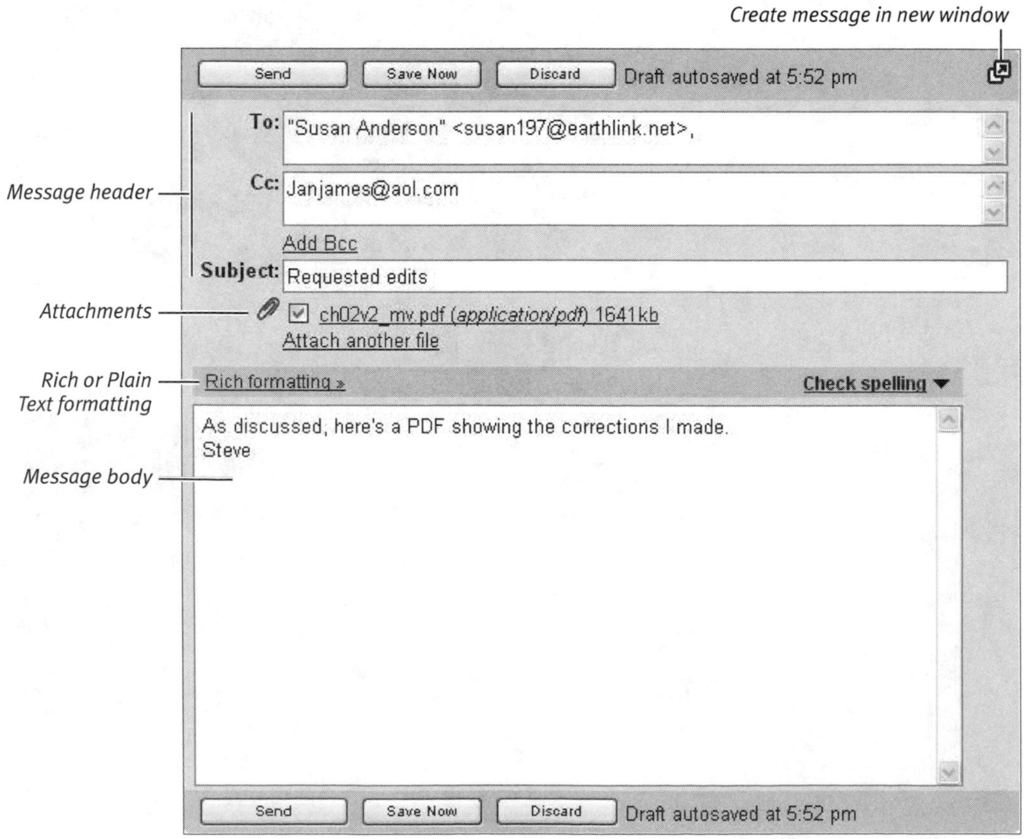

Figure 5.4 You create messages in this pane.

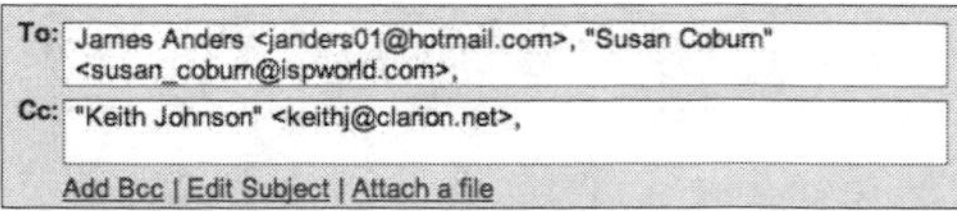

Figure 5.5 Optionally, a message can also contain Cc and/or Bcc recipients.

Selecting a Recipient Type

In any message, you can have any combination of To, Cc, and Bcc recipients. If you're not sure who should go where, the following may be helpful:

- Individuals in the To line are normally the primary recipients.
- Cc recipients are people who you want to copy on the message. When emailing a coworker, for instance, you might Cc a supervisor.
- Make people Bcc recipients when you want their names to be hidden from all other recipients.

Contrary to popular belief, a message is not required to have a To recipient. For example, when sending a joke or article to many people, you could make them *all* Bcc recipients.

Creating a New Message

Creating new messages is one of the most basic email activities.

To create a new message from scratch:

1. Click the Compose Mail link on the left side of the window.

   A new message pane appears.

2. *Optional:* If you're more comfortable creating messages in a separate window (as is done in most email programs), click the New Window icon (see Figure 5.4).
3. In the To box, specify the email address of the primary recipient by doing one of the following:
   - Start typing the name or email address. As you type, Gmail presents a list of possible matches drawn from your Contacts list (see Figure 5.3). Click to select a contact.
   - If none of the proposed contacts is the one you want, ignore them and finish typing the email address.
   - Paste a complete email address into the box.
4. *Optional:* To enter more To addresses, click to the right of the last To address and repeat Step 3.
5. *Optional:* You can also include *Cc* (carbon copy) or *Bcc* (blind carbon copy) recipients. Click Add Cc or Add Bcc, click in the Cc or Bcc box that appears (**Figure 5.5**), and perform Steps 3–4.
6. Enter a Subject to identify the message.
7. *Optional:* Gmail messages default to Rich Text formatting. To create an unformatted, single font message, click the Plain text link.

continues on next page

8. Press Tab or click in the message box, and type your message.
9. When you've finished typing the message, click one of the following buttons at the top or bottom of the message window (**Figure 5.6**):
   - ▲ **Send.** Click this button to send the message now.
   - ▲ **Save Now.** Click this button if you want to edit the message before sending it or wish to send it at a later time. The message will be stored in Drafts until you send it.
   - ▲ **Discard.** If you decide not to send or save the current message, click Discard to throw it away.

Figure 5.6 When you're done composing, click one of these buttons.

✔ Tips

- Although the message creation steps are presented in linear fashion, you can perform them in any order that's convenient.
- When there are multiple recipients in the To, Cc, or Bcc boxes, all addresses are separated by commas (see Figure 5.5).
- If you want to attach one or more files to the message, see "Attaching Files," later in this chapter. For information on using the spell checker, see "Using the Spell Checker," also in this chapter.
- To use Rich Text formatting to create, reply to, or forward messages, you must be in Gmail's standard view and be using a browser that supports this feature.
- You can copy text from other documents, Web pages, and email messages, and then paste it into a message you're writing, replying to, or forwarding. When pasted into a Rich Text message, much of the original formatting is retained. When pasted into a Plain Text message, all character formatting is discarded.

Creating a Message in a New Window

You already know that you can compose a message in a new window by clicking the New Window icon (see Figure 5.4). But there's another way to open a new composition window that saves a step in this process. Hold down Shift as you click the Compose Mail, Reply, Reply to all, or Forward link.

Figure 5.7 Click Reply to write a response to the current message.

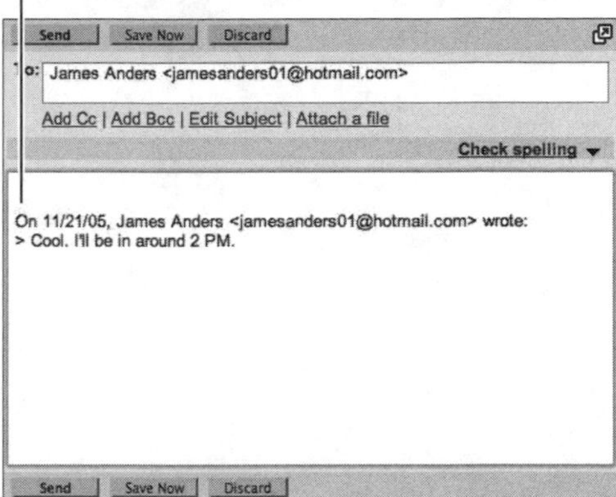

Figure 5.8 A reply pane opens beneath the original message.

Replying to a Message

When you receive email from someone and want to respond, you'll normally create a *reply* to the message rather than composing an entirely new message.

The Subject of a reply is generated by Gmail and is in the form Re: *original subject*. This serves two purposes. First, it lets the recipient know that you are replying to a particular message that she or he sent to you. Second, Gmail uses the Subject to determine whether a message is on a new topic or is part of a conversation.

To create a reply:

1. Open the message to which you want to send a reply.
2. Click the Reply link at the bottom of the message (**Figure 5.7**).

   A copy of the message appears, addressed to the original author as the main recipient (**Figure 5.8**). The author's original text is marked with > characters.
3. *Optional:* You can specify additional recipients by doing any of the following:
   - ▲ To create an additional To recipient, type a comma after the author's address, start typing the new person's name or address, and then select the recipient from the drop-down list. (If the person isn't in the list, finish typing his or her email address.)
   - ▲ Click Add Cc or Add Bcc to add carbon copy or blind carbon copy recipients.
4. *Optional:* To change the Subject, click Edit Subject.

   A Subject box appears in which you can make any desired changes.

continues on next page

5. *Optional:* Gmail messages default to Rich Text formatting. To create an unformatted, single font message, click the Plain text link (**Figure 5.9**).

6. Edit the quoted text as desired, removing any extraneous material.

7. Type your reply. Gmail provides space above the quoted text for a reply.

8. When you've finished typing the message, click one of the following buttons at the top or bottom of the message window (see Figure 5.6):

   ▲ **Send.** Click this button to send the message now.

   ▲ **Save Now.** Click this button if you want to edit the message before sending it or wish to send it at a later time. The message will be stored in Drafts until you send it.

   ▲ **Discard.** If you decide not to send or save the current message, click Discard to throw it away.

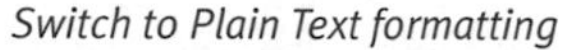

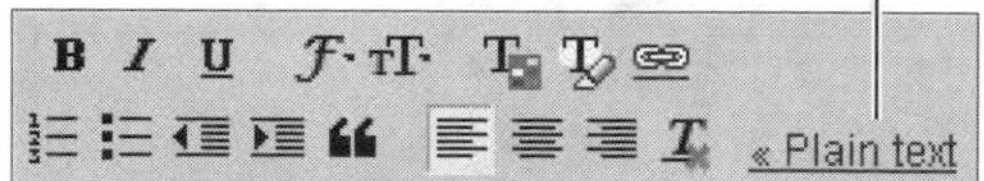

Figure 5.9 To format the reply as a Plain Text message, click the Plain text link.

✓ Tips

- When Gmail quotes text from a previous message, it does so in *levels*. A single quote (>) denotes text from the most recent message. The further removed from the most recent message, the more quote characters precede the text.
- The amount of quoted material you leave in a reply is up to you. In general, it's sufficient to retain only the relevant text to which you're responding.
- You can attach one or multiple files to a reply, if you wish. For information, see "Attaching Files," later in this chapter.
- Unless you're in a rush, it's a good idea to check your spelling prior to sending a message. For help, see "Using the Spell Checker," also in this chapter.

Reply vs. Reply to All

You'll note that some messages also have a *Reply to all* link. Use Reply and Reply to all as follows:

- To reply only to the person from whom you've received the message, use Reply. This is the command you will use for most replies.
- To send a reply to a message's author, as well as to all other people listed in the To and Cc lines, use Reply to all.

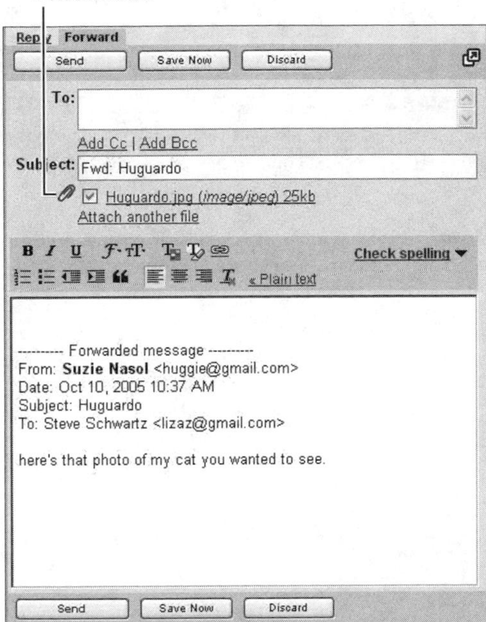

Figure 5.10 When forwarding a message, the original text is automatically copied into the message window. Attachments are also forwarded.

Forwarding a Message

Forwarding a message is similar to replying to a message. However, the recipient is always someone other than the message's author. You use forwarding to pass along a received message to other people. For example, if you receive an interesting bit of family news, you might forward it to other relatives. A forwarded message is indicated by a Fwd: prefix added to the Subject.

To forward a message to others:

1. Open the message you want to forward.
2. Click the Forward link at the bottom of the message (see Figure 5.7).

   A copy of the original message appears (**Figure 5.10**). The text is preceded by a —Forwarded message— line.
3. In the To box, specify the email address of the primary recipient. Do one of the following:
   - Start typing the name or email address. As you type, Gmail presents a list of possible matches drawn from your Contacts list (see Figure 5.3). Click to select a contact.
   - If none of the proposed contacts is the one you want, ignore them and finish typing the email address.
   - Paste a complete email address into the box.
4. *Optional:* To enter more To addresses, click to the right of the last To address and repeat Step 3.
5. *Optional:* You can also include *Cc* (carbon copy) or *Bcc* (blind carbon copy) recipients. Click Add Cc or Add Bcc, click in the Cc or Bcc box that appears (see Figure 5.5), and perform Steps 3–4.

continues on next page

6. *Optional:* Edit the subject, if you like.
7. *Optional:* Gmail messages default to Rich Text formatting. To create an unformatted, single font message, click the Plain text link (see Figure 5.9).
8. Edit the forwarded text, if desired. You can also add your own message in the space before the material you're forwarding.
9. When you've finished typing the message, click one of the following buttons at the top or bottom of the message window (see Figure 5.6):
   - ▲ **Send.** Click this button to send the message now.
   - ▲ **Save Now.** Click this button if you want to edit the message before sending it or wish to send it at a later time. The message will be stored in Drafts until you send it.
   - ▲ **Discard.** If you decide not to send or save the current message, click Discard to throw it away.

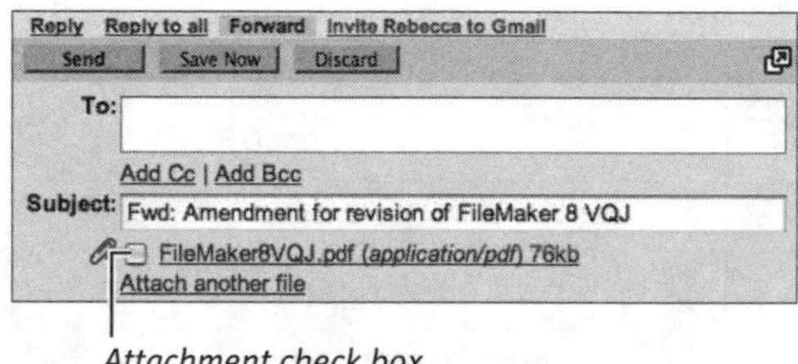

Figure 5.11 Remove the check mark from any original attachment that you do not want to forward.

✔ Tips

- When forwarding a message, take the time to strip out other people's email addresses from the forwarded material.
- Forwarding attachments is optional. To prevent a given attachment from being forwarded with the message, remove its check mark (**Figure 5.11**).
- You can add other attachments to a forwarded message, if you wish. For instructions, see "Attaching Files," later in this chapter.

Formatting Messages

When you want to use special fonts, character sizes, styles, colors, and paragraph formatting, you can create a Rich Text message that's similar to a word processing document. Most email clients are capable of displaying such messages.

Gmail supports character and paragraph formatting as follows:

- *Character formatting* is applied to selected text within a paragraph. Options include boldface, italic, underlining, font, font size, text color, links, and highlighting.
- *Paragraph formatting* affects entire paragraphs. Options include numbered and bulleted lists, indents, quotes, and alignment.

To create a formatted message:

1. *Do one of the following:*
   - ▲ Click Compose Mail to create a new message.
   - ▲ When reading a message, click the Reply, Reply to all, or Forward link beneath the message.

   By default, Gmail messages are formatted (Rich Text).
2. Click icons on the formatting toolbar (**Figure 5.12**) to apply formatting to selected text or prior to typing new text.

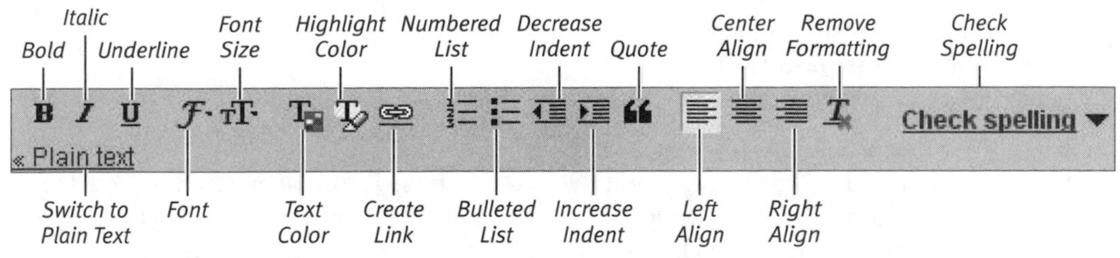

Figure 5.12 To set formatting options, click these icons on the formatting toolbar.

✔ Tips

- Multiple character formatting options can be applied to the same text. For example, you could apply boldface, italic, and blue color to a word or phrase.
- When applying formatting as you type, most options work as on/off combinations. For instance, click the Bold icon, type a word or phrase in boldface, and then click the Bold icon again to return to normal, non-bold text. Similarly, to end a bulleted or numbered list, click the bulleted or numbered list icon again.
- Gmail allows you to embed many types of clickable links in a message, although you're likely to only use *http:* (URL/Web address) and *mailto:* (email address). If you type a valid Web or email address in a message, Gmail will normally recognize it and format it with a blue underline.
- You can also create a link from text that isn't a valid link, such as:

  ```
  Click here to visit my Web site.
  ```

  Select the text that will serve as the link, and then click the Link toolbar icon. In the Hyperlink dialog box that appears (**Figure 5.13**), select a link type from the Type drop-down list and type the link address following the prefix that appears in the URL box.
- Use the quote option to mark selected paragraphs as a quote from another email message, a passage from a book or article, or a statement by a famous person, for example. (You must select the *entire* paragraph when applying quote formatting to text.)
- If you've started a Rich Text message and decide that formatting isn't necessary, you don't have to start over. Just click the Plain Text link.

Figure 5.13 Create a hyperlink from selected text by specifying the link information in this dialog box. When opened in most email clients, the link will be clickable.

- To remove formatting from selected text, click the Remove Formatting toolbar icon.

Your message has been discarded. Undo discard

Figure 5.14 If you discard a draft you are viewing, this message appears.

Figure 5.15 When Gmail autosaves a message in progress, a notification appears beside these buttons.

Figure 5.16 If you abandon a message in progress, this dialog box appears.

✔ Tips

- Gmail *automatically* saves messages in progress every few minutes (**Figure 5.15**). If you quit without sending a message, you'll usually find it in the Drafts section.
- If you try to switch to another Gmail section while editing a new message or a draft in which the changes have not been saved or autosaved, a dialog box appears (**Figure 5.16**). Click OK to discard all changes you made, or click Cancel if you want to continue working on the message.
- You can also delete a draft by clicking its check box in the message list and then clicking Discard Drafts. Note, however, that such deletions are irreversible.

Working with Drafts

It isn't always possible (or necessary) to complete an email message in one sitting. You can save a message in progress as a *draft*, storing it in the Drafts section until you're ready to complete and/or send it.

To save a message as a draft:

◆ While composing a new message, writing a reply, or forwarding a message, click the Save Now button above or below the message.

The message is stored in Drafts. You can continue working on the message, perform other Gmail activities, visit another Web site, or close your browser.

To view, edit, or send a draft:

1. Click the Drafts link (on the left side of any Gmail page).
2. Click the header of the draft you want to edit or view.
3. Make any necessary edits.
4. *Do one of the following:*
   - ▲ To save the edited draft, click the Save Now button. (The message will remain in Drafts.)
   - ▲ To send the message, click the Send button. The message is sent and moved from Drafts into Sent Mail.
   - ▲ To delete the draft, click Discard. If you wish to restore the deleted draft, immediately click Undo discard (**Figure 5.14**).

Attaching Files

Like other email clients, Gmail allows you to attach files to messages. You can send photos, movie clips, word processing documents, or worksheets, for example. The only file type which you are prohibited from sending is a Windows *.exe* (executable) file; viruses are often spread in this manner. After Gmail has encoded your attachments for mailing, their total size must be less than 10 MB.

To attach a file to a message (Mac):

1. When creating, forwarding, or replying to a message, click Attach a file.

   In a new or forwarded message, the link is beneath the Subject box; in a reply, it is beneath the To box.

2. Click the Choose File button that appears (**Figure 5.17**).

   A file pane appears.

3. Navigate to the drive and folder that contains the file you wish to attach to the message. Select the file and click Choose (**Figure 5.18**).

   The path to the chosen file is displayed, and the file is uploaded to Gmail.

4. *Optional:* To attach an additional file to the message, click Attach another file. Repeat Steps 2–4.

✔ Tips

- Prior to sending, you can remove any attachment by quickly clicking the remove link or by clearing its check box. Otherwise, the upload finishes and the file is attached to the message (**Figure 5.19**).

- When replying to a message that contains an attachment, you can enclose the original attachment by clicking Include original attachments. (This isn't recommended unless the author asks for them.)

Figure 5.17 When you click Attach a file, a Choose File button appears. Click the button to select a file to attach to this message.

Figure 5.18 Select a file to attach to the message and click the Choose button.

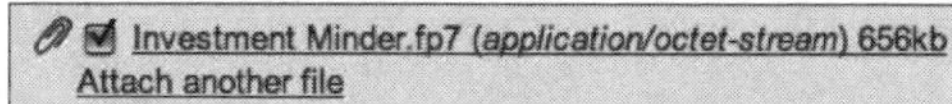

Figure 5.19 The chosen file's name and size are shown.

Figure 5.20 To add an attachment to the message, click Attach a file.

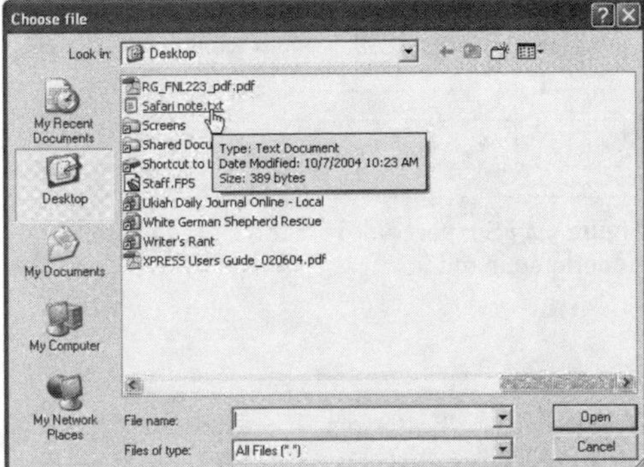

Figure 5.21 Select the file you wish to attach.

To attach a file to a message (Windows):

1. When creating, forwarding, or replying to a message, click Attach a file (**Figure 5.20**).

   In a new or forwarded message, the link is beneath the Subject box; in a reply, it is beneath the To box.

2. In the Choose file dialog box that appears (**Figure 5.21**), navigate to the drive and folder that contains the file you want to attach to the message, and select the file. (The dialog box should immediately close. If it doesn't, click the Open button.)

   The path to the chosen file is displayed, and the file is uploaded to Gmail.

3. *Optional:* To attach an additional file to the message, click Attach another file. Repeat Steps 2–3.

✔ Tips

- Prior to sending, you can remove any attachment by quickly clicking the remove link or by clearing its check box. Otherwise, the upload finishes and the file is attached to the message (see Figure 5.19).
- When replying to a message that contains an attachment, you can enclose the original attachment by clicking Include original attachments. (This isn't recommended unless the author asks for them.)

Using the Spell Checker

Before sending a message you're composing, replying to, or forwarding, it's a good practice to check your spelling.

By default, the spell checker uses the language specified for Gmail's interface (see the discussion in Chapter 1 about the General tab of Mail Settings). To select a different language to spell check this message, click the down-arrow beside Check spelling (**Figure 5.22**).

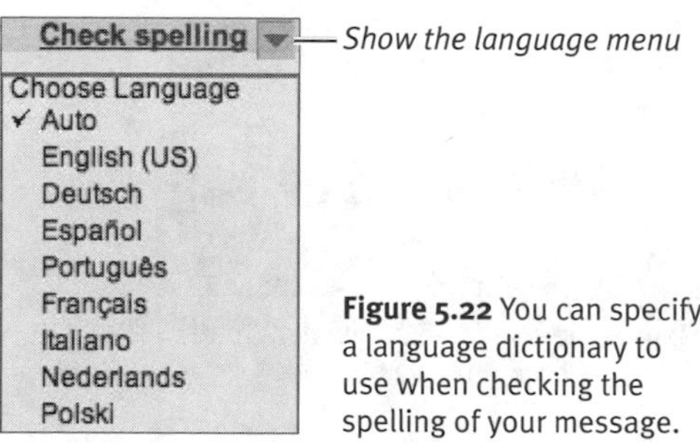

Figure 5.22 You can specify a language dictionary to use when checking the spelling of your message.

To check spelling for a message:

1. To initiate a spell check, click Check spelling.

   Suspect words are underlined and colored red (**Figure 5.23**).

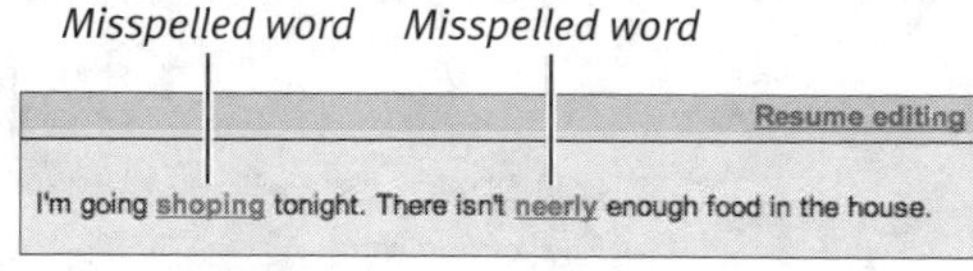

Figure 5.23 Suspect words in the message body are underlined in red.

2. Click each underlined word. You can then do any of the following:
   - ▲ Select the correct spelling from the drop-down list that appears (**Figure 5.24**). The selected word replaces the original one.
   - ▲ To manually correct the word's spelling, select Edit from the drop-down list. The suspect word is presented in a text box in which you can make the necessary corrections (**Figure 5.25**).
   - ▲ If you believe that the word is already correct, click away from the menu to leave the word unchanged.

Figure 5.24 You can select a replacement word from the drop-down list.

Figure 5.25 If the suggested spellings aren't correct, you can manually edit the word.

3. Click Resume editing.

   Your spelling corrections are incorporated into the message.

✔ Tip

- Mac OS X (Tiger) users can use the built-in dictionary. If you aren't sure whether you're using a word correctly, select it, Ctrl-click it, and choose Look Up in Dictionary from the contextual menu. The word's definition appears (**Figure 5.26**).

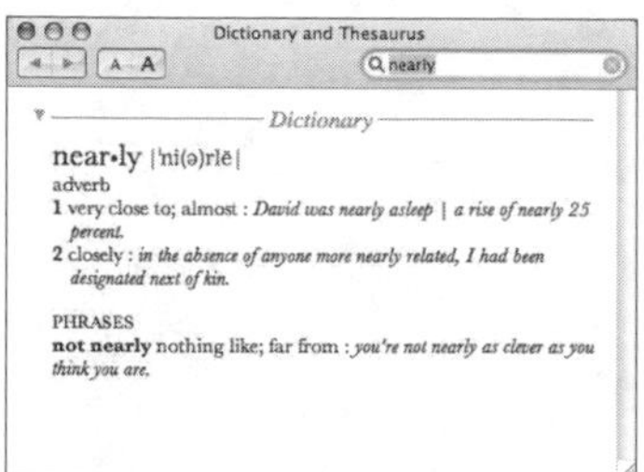

Figure 5.26 Mac OS X Tiger users can view the definition of any word.

Email Etiquette

Just like any other form of communication, there are some commonly accepted rules for creating email messages. The following suggestions may prove helpful to you.

- *Don't use all caps.* The day of caps-only Teletypes ended almost 30 years ago. Messages consisting of capital letters only are difficult to read and may be misinterpreted as *yelling*. The upper- and lowercase letters on your keyboard are there for a good reason.
- *Quote only as much text as necessary.* When replying to a lengthy message, quote only the text to which you're responding. For example, if you're replying to a newsy message but are only commenting on a recipe that was included, eliminate all the other quoted text. Doing so will keep your messages concise and make it easier for the recipient to understand which material you're commenting on.
- *Don't forward messages within messages.* You'll occasionally receive a forwarded message with an attachment that—when opened—reveals yet another attachment. After opening a dozen such attachments, you *may* find the actual message.

  If you want to forward this message to others, don't just click Forward. Copy the actual text to be forwarded, paste it into a new message, and then send *that* message rather than the original. Doing so will make the message send faster (since it will be much smaller) and will save your friends some aggravation.

continues on next page

- *Be selective when forwarding messages.* New users tend to forward many messages. And when they do, the messages often go to every person in their Contacts list. Recognize that not everyone shares your sense of humor or political leaning. Be selective when choosing which messages to forward, as well as which people will be recipients.

  Be especially selective when forwarding chain letters. Many are Internet frauds, hoaxes, and jokes. To learn which email messages are known hoaxes, visit a hoax-buster site, such as *www.snopes.com*.

- *Know your audience.* Internet shorthand (such as typing *u* for *you* and *ur* for *your*) has become commonplace, but is best reserved for casual correspondence. Some people will accept it or think you're cute, others will overlook it, and still others will think you're a twit.

- *There's a reason a spell checker is included.* If spelling isn't your forte (or you don't know what *forte* means), use the spell checker before sending a message. Even if you aren't a great speller, you can impersonate one.

Managing the Mail

There's more to using an email application than composing and reading messages. You'll also want to *manage* your email, making some messages more accessible and removing ones you don't want to keep, for example.

In this chapter, you'll learn how to:

- Change the status of incoming messages from read to unread (and vice versa)
- Mark special or important messages with a star
- Create labels to organize your messages according to sender, content, or some other criteria
- Delete unwanted messages, permanently removing them from Gmail
- Archive messages that are worth keeping, but aren't important enough to store in your Inbox
- Deal with nuisance and dangerous email (spam, phishing, and viruses)

Marking Mail as Read or Unread

One of the simplest ways to manage your mail happens automatically. Whenever you receive a new message, its message header is displayed in boldface in all message lists. After you open the message, the boldface is replaced by normal type. This convention allows you to quickly scan any message list and identify the unread messages.

You can also *manually* change a message's read/unread status. I routinely mark weekly sales messages from computer suppliers as read, for example, because I consider reading them optional. Similarly, if I want to ensure that I eventually respond to a message I've read, I may set its status to unread.

To change a message's status:

1. In any message list, select one or more messages and/or conversations.
2. From the More Actions drop-down menu, choose Mark as read or Mark as unread (**Figure 6.1**).

   All selected messages and conversations are set to the chosen status.

✔ Tips

- When the selected items have different statuses (some read and some unread), both status choices will be listed in the More Actions drop-down menu. When the selected items have the same status, only the opposite choice will be listed.
- When you change the status of a conversation, all messages in the conversation are set to the new status. You cannot selectively change the status of individual messages in a conversation.
- You can also change the status of a message or conversation you're reading.

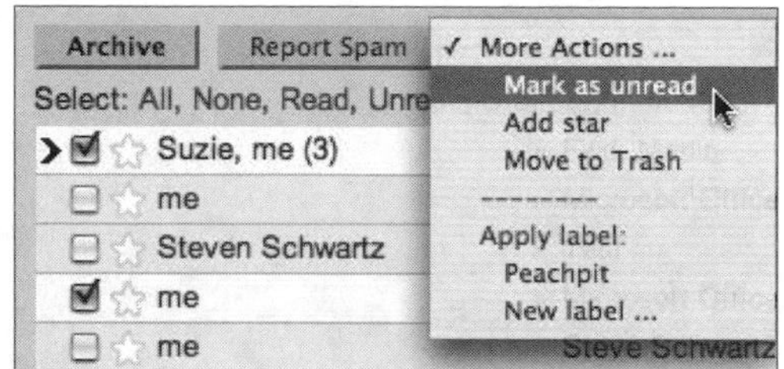

Figure 6.1 To change the status of selected messages, choose a new status from the More Actions menu.

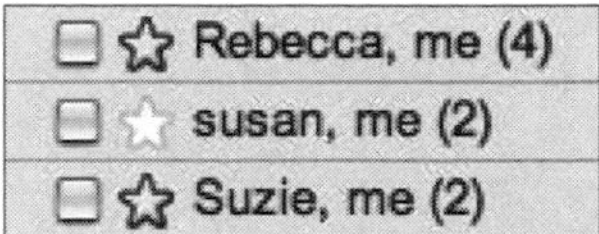

Figure 6.2 Important messages and conversations can be marked with a yellow star.

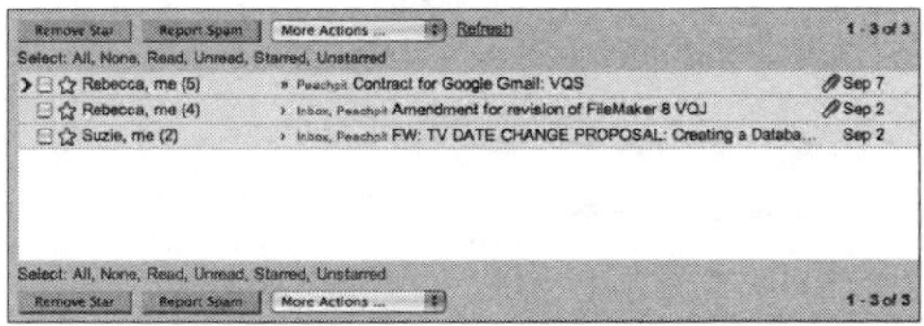

Figure 6.3 To restrict the current view to only starred messages and conversations (shown here), click the Starred link to the left of any message list.

Select: All, None, Read, Unread, Starred, Unstarred

Figure 6.4 You can select all starred or unstarred messages by clicking a link.

Marking Messages with a Star

Gmail provides a method of quickly distinguishing critical or special messages from the rest. You can *star* them. Each starred message (**Figure 6.2**) is marked with a bright yellow star. Starred messages are also listed by date in the Starred section of Gmail (**Figure 6.3**).

To apply or remove a star:

- *Do one of the following:*
  - Click the star symbol to the left of the message or conversation header.

    If the message or conversation has no star, one is applied. If the message or conversation has a star, it is removed.
  - Select the messages and conversations whose star status you want to change. From the More Actions drop-down menu, choose Add star or Remove star.

✔ Tips

- You can also apply a star based on a filter. See Chapter 7 for information on filter actions.
- To quickly select all starred or unstarred messages, click the appropriate Select link (**Figure 6.4**) above or below the current message list.

Using Labels

A *label* is the Gmail equivalent of a mail folder in other email applications. By applying a label to selected messages and conversations, you can view them all in one convenient spot. Examples of labels include:

- *Kinston Associates* (for work-related messages or ones from an important client)
- *Gmail VQS* (for mail related to the writing of this book)
- *First Lutheran* (for church-related mail)
- *Term Paper* (for a school assignment)
- *Friends* (for messages from select friends)

You can manually apply labels to selected messages and conversations, as well as apply them automatically to incoming messages as the result of a Gmail filter.

To create a label without specifying an initial set of messages:

1. In the Labels box on the left side of the window, click Edit labels.

   The Labels tab of the Mail Settings window appears (**Figure 6.5**).
2. Enter the label's name in the Create a new label box and click Create.

   The new label is added.

To create a label for selected messages:

1. In any message list, select the messages and conversations to which you want to apply the new label.
2. From the More Actions drop-down menu, choose New label.
3. In the dialog box that appears, name the new label and click OK (**Figure 6.6**).

   The label is created and applied to the selected messages.

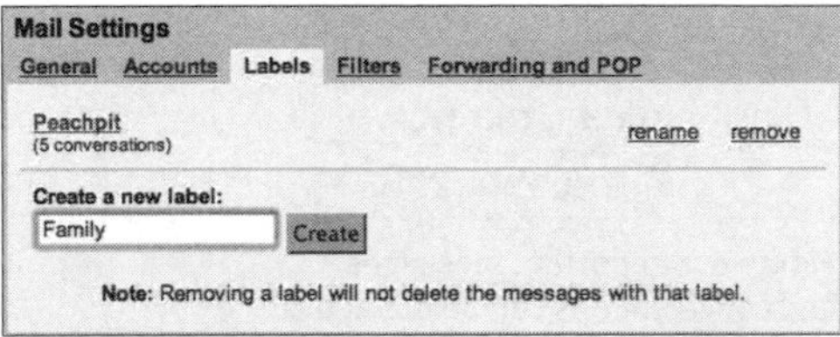

Figure 6.5 You can create, rename, or delete labels on the Labels tab of the Mail Settings window.

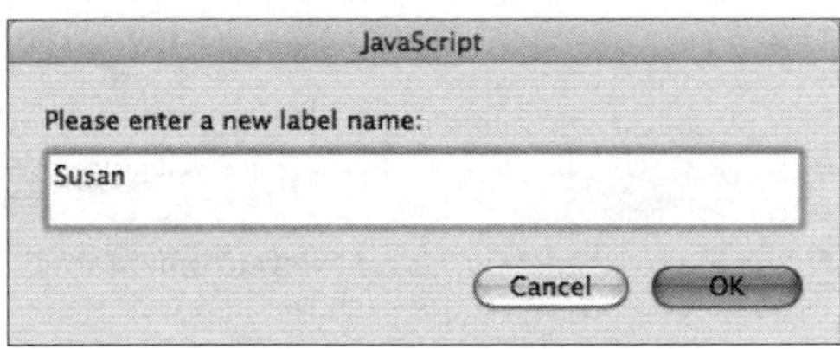

Figure 6.6 Name the new label and click OK.

USING LABELS

Figure 6.7 Choose a label to apply from the More Actions drop-down menu.

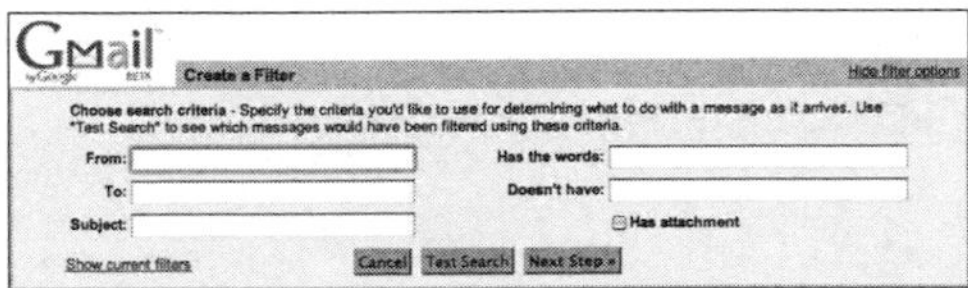

Figure 6.8 Enter filter criteria in this pane.

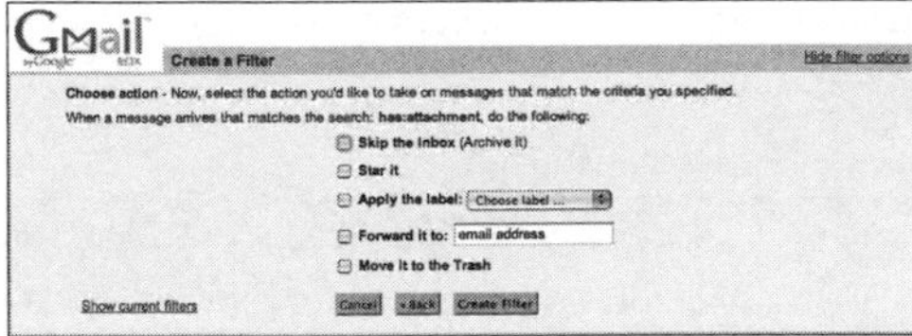

Figure 6.9 Click the Apply the label check box, select a label from the drop-down list, and click Create Filter.

To apply a label to selected messages:

1. Select one or more messages or conversations in any message list.
2. From the More Actions drop-down menu, choose the label to apply from the Apply label submenu (**Figure 6.7**).

   The label is applied to the item or items.

To apply a label using a filter:

1. Click the Create a filter link at the top of any Gmail page.

   The Create a Filter pane appears at the top of the page (**Figure 6.8**).
2. Enter the criteria that will be used to identify new messages to which the filter should be applied.
3. *Optional:* To test the criteria on existing messages, click Test Search.

   The message list will show all messages that meet the filter's criteria.
4. Click Next Step.

   The Choose action section of the Create a Filter pane appears (**Figure 6.9**).
5. Click the Apply the label check box.
6. From the Choose label drop-down list, select the name of an existing label or select New label to create a label for this filter.
7. Click the Create Filter button.

   The new filter is added to the list on the Filters tab of the Mail Settings page. New messages that meet the filter's criteria will automatically have the specified label applied to them. (To learn more about creating and editing filters, see Chapter 7.)

To remove a label:

1. Select a message or conversation in any message list.

   If you're certain that several messages or conversations share the same label, you can select multiple items.

2. From the More Actions drop-down menu, choose the label to remove from the Remove label submenu (**Figure 6.10**).

   The label is removed from the selected item or items.

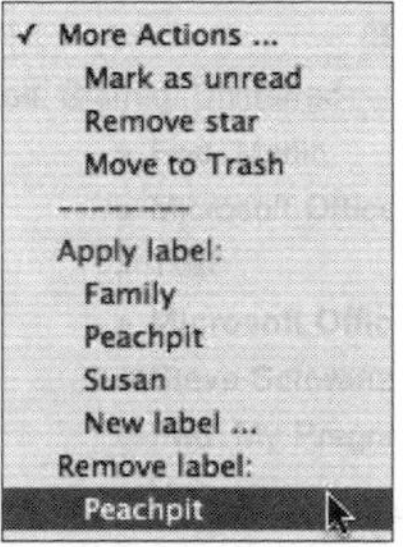

Figure 6.10 Choose the label to remove from the More Actions drop-down menu.

To rename or delete a label:

1. Click the Settings link at the top of any Gmail page.

   The Mail Settings page appears.

2. Click the Labels link (**Figure 6.11**).

3. *Do one of the following:*
   - ▲ To delete a label, click its Remove link.
   - ▲ To change a label's name, click its Rename link. Change the name in the dialog box that appears (**Figure 6.12**) and click OK.

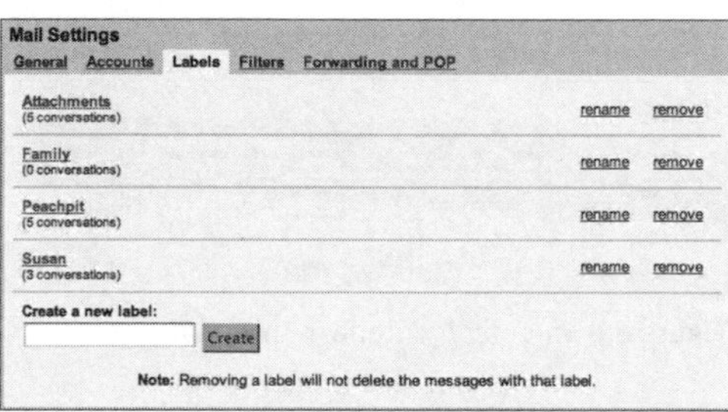

Figure 6.11 To rename or remove (delete) a label, click a link to the right of the label's name.

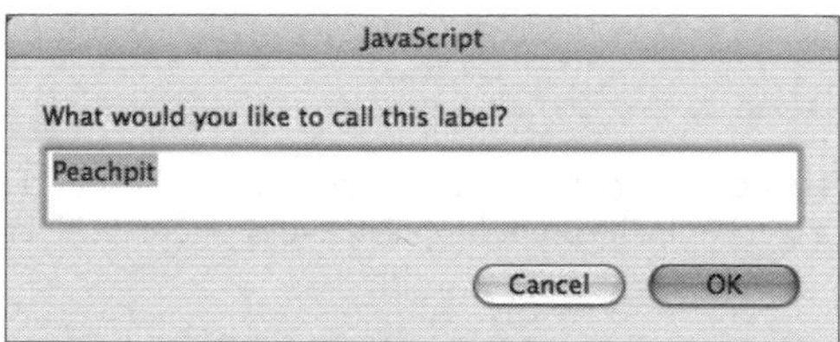

Figure 6.12 Edit or replace the label name, and then click OK.

✔ Tips

- You can apply *multiple* labels to any message or conversation.
- You can also apply or remove labels while reading a message or conversation. Choose the appropriate command from the More Actions drop-down menu.

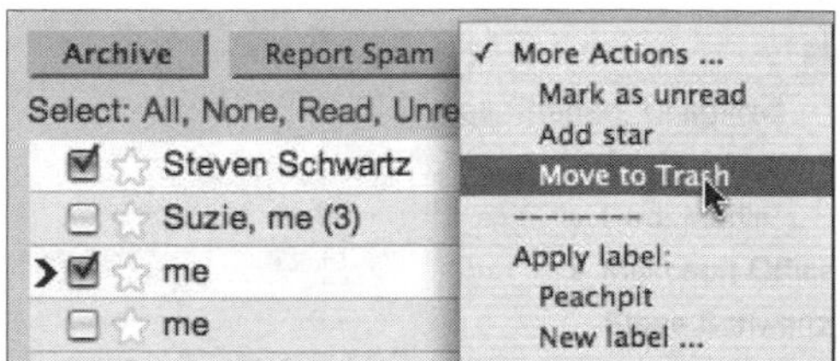

Figure 6.13 To delete a message or conversation, click its check box and choose Move to Trash.

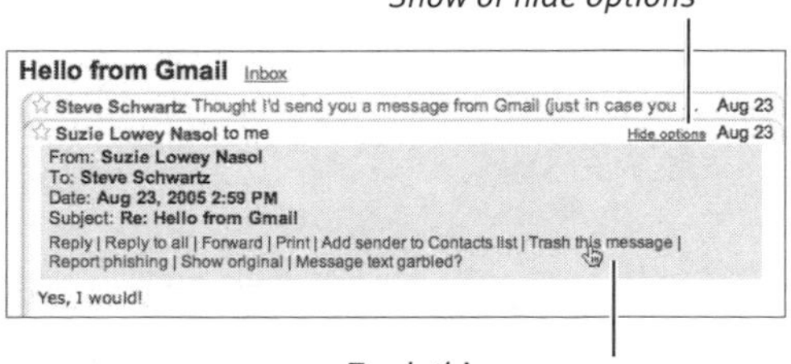

Figure 6.14 To delete a message within a conversation, expand the message, click More options, and then click Trash this message.

Delete Forever button

Figure 6.15 Items in the Trash aren't actually deleted until you confirm by clicking Delete Forever.

Deleting and Archiving Mail

Although Gmail provides 2 GB of storage per account, it's unlikely that you'll want to keep *every* message you send and receive. The presence of hundreds of trivial messages can make it difficult to find the important ones.

One way of managing your email is to simply move unimportant messages out of the way—out of the Inbox and Sent Mail sections. Gmail provides two ways for you to accomplish this:

- Delete messages and conversations
- Archive messages and conversations

Deleting messages

Deleting a message moves it from its permanent location (Inbox or Sent Mail) into the Trash. Deleted items remain in the Trash until you click Delete Forever or for 30 days, after which Gmail automatically deletes them.

To delete a message or conversation:

1. *Do one of the following:*
   - In any message list, select messages and/or conversations by clicking each one's check box. Choose Move to Trash from the More Actions drop-down menu (**Figure 6.13**).
   - To select a single message within a conversation, open the conversation, expand the message so it can be read, click More options, and then click Trash this message (**Figure 6.14**).

   The message is moved into the Trash.
2. To permanently delete a message in the Trash, select it (by clicking its check box) and click Delete Forever (**Figure 6.15**).

Archiving messages

Archiving isn't as drastic as deletion. It merely moves a message or conversation out of the Inbox. If you later want to read an archived message, it can be found in the All Mail section, as well as in any sections in which it was previously stored, such as labels or Starred.

Note: Mail in Sent Mail can't be archived nor can individual messages within a conversation.

To archive a message or conversation:

1. In a message list, select messages and/or conversations by clicking each one's check box.
2. Click the Archive button or choose Archive from the More Actions drop-down menu.

   The selected messages and conversations are removed from the Inbox. They can still be read in All Mail, as well as in any other section in which they were originally stored.

✔ Tips

- Deletion is a two-step process. If you change your mind about deleting a message or conversation, select it in the Trash and click Move to Inbox (see Figure 6.15). The item will be restored to the Inbox or Sent Mail —wherever it was originally stored.
- When you select an item in a message list, you're simultaneously selecting it in *every* message list that contains the item. Regardless of the message list in which you select a message or conversation, moving it to the Trash deletes *all* copies.
- When you delete an item in Sent Mail, a warning sometimes appears (**Figure 6.16**). If the message really *is* part of an existing conversation, heed the warning.

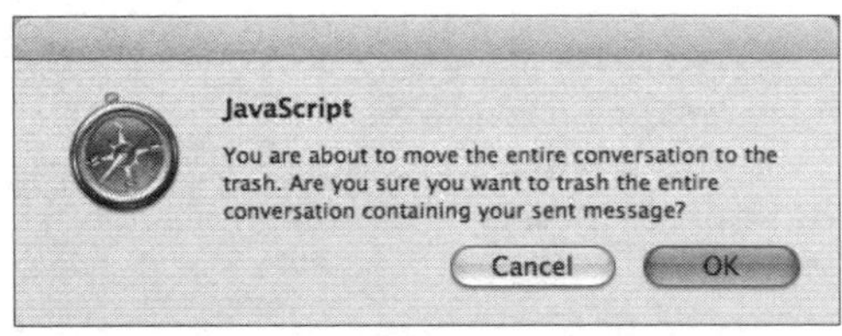

Figure 6.16 When you attempt to delete an item in Sent Mail, this warning may appear.

Date: **Nov 15, 2005 4:43 PM**
Subject: **Your PayPal account**
Reply | Reply to all | Forward | Print | Add sender to Contacts list |
Trash this message | Report phishing | Show original | Message text garbled?

Click to report phishing

Figure 6.17 If Gmail misses a phishing attempt, you can report it by clicking this link in the open message.

Handling Viruses, Phishing, and Spam

Unfortunately, there are a lot of people who seem intent on making the Internet a dangerous place for the rest of us. They inundate our email accounts with *spam* (junk mail), *phishing* (fraudulent messages to trick us into giving them Web site passwords or credit card information), and *viruses* (file attachments that surreptitiously install destructive software on our computers).

Viruses

Gmail does not perform a virus scan on incoming or outgoing mail. However, it automatically removes any attachment that is a Windows *.exe* (executable) file. For additional virus protection, you should install one of the popular anti-virus applications, such as Norton AntiVirus.

Phishing

Gmail attempts to detect incoming phishing messages. If you receive such an email, a warning is displayed with the message. However, common sense is still the best protection against phishing. Reputable Web sites will never send emails asking for your account or credit card information. Similarly, if an email link directs you to a Web form requesting that information, it is usually best to ignore it. (This is a common phishing trick.)

To manage phishing messages:

- *Do any of the following:*
  - If Gmail incorrectly classifies a message as phishing, click Report Not Phishing.
  - To report a phishing attempt that Gmail missed, open the message, click Show options, and click Report phishing (**Figure 6.17**).

Spam

While not a threat, spam is definitely an annoyance. Having to wade through unwanted advertising emails to find your personal and business messages is time consuming.

Messages that Gmail classifies as spam are automatically routed to the Spam folder. The following step lists explain how to work with spam in Gmail.

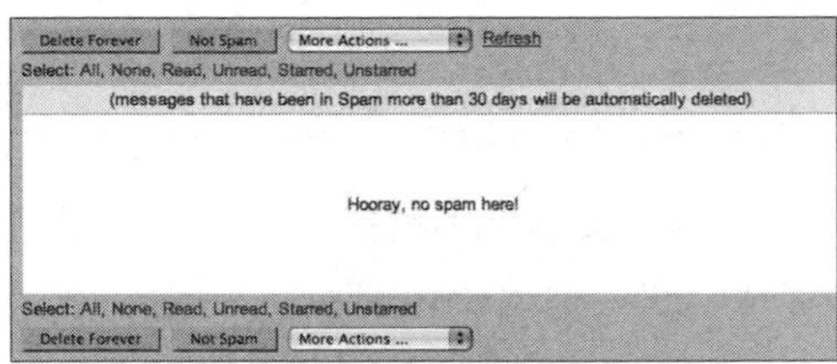

Figure 6.18 The Spam section.

To manage messages in Spam:

1. Click the Spam link on the left side of any Gmail page.

   The Spam section appears (**Figure 6.18**).

2. *Do any of the following:*
   - ▲ To delete one or more selected messages, click Delete Forever.
   - ▲ To reclassify one or more selected messages as not being spam, click Not Spam. The sender is automatically added as a new contact and the message is moved to your Inbox.

     If you've opened the message or it's part of a conversation, a Not Spam button will be displayed there, too.

All Gmail message lists that can contain incoming mail have a Report Spam button or More Actions command. By reporting a message as spam, you help improve the accuracy of Gmail's spam detection.

To report a message as spam:

1. Select or open the spam message.
2. *Do one of the following:*
   - ▲ Click the Report Spam button above or below the message list.
   - ▲ If there's no Report Spam button, choose Report as spam from the More Actions drop-down menu.

7 Filtering and Searching for Mail

When your Inbox, Sent Mail, and All Mail begin to bulge, it can be tough to quickly find a particular message. Rather than simply relying on your memory, you can use Gmail's search features. As you'll learn in this chapter, you can perform simple searches by typing search text into a box. Or you can perform more advanced searches, such as limiting the search to the Subject, for example. Because Gmail is a Google product, you can even perform Google searches from within Gmail.

This chapter will also show you how to create filters that will automatically assign a star, apply a label, delete, or forward certain incoming messages.

The Search Pane

Basic searches are performed in the *search pane* (**Figure 7.1**), found at the top of most Gmail pages. You can perform the following types of searches in the search pane:

- Search Gmail messages for the occurrence of the search string in a recipient or sender's name, email address, subject, or message text
- Perform an advanced search by clicking Show search options or by including advanced search operators in the search text (see Appendix B)
- Restrict an advanced search to certain sections of Gmail, such as the Inbox, Read Mail, or a label
- Perform a Google Web search

✔ Tip

- If Gmail's keyboard shortcuts are enabled (see Chapter 1 and Appendix A), you can press / to move the cursor into the search box.

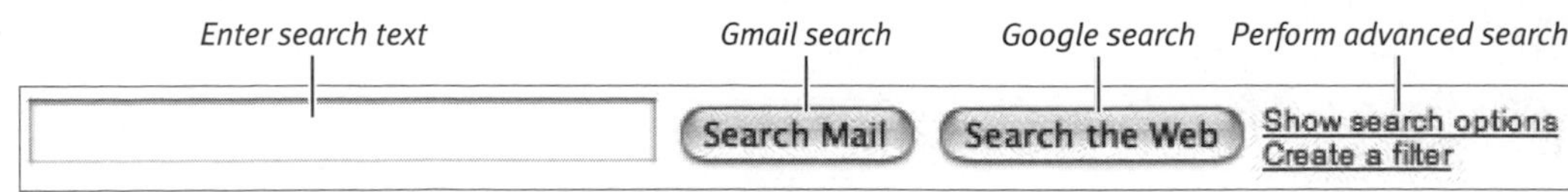

Figure 7.1 Email and Web searches are conducted in the search pane.

Figure 7.2 Enter one or more search words and click Search Mail.

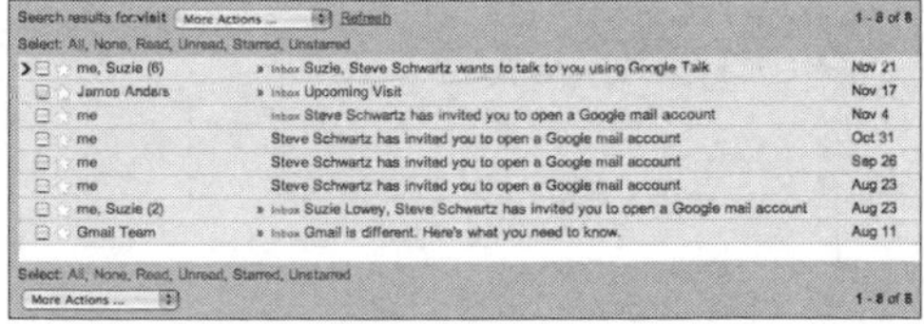

Figure 7.3 Matching messages and conversations appear as a new list.

Performing a Basic Search

The quickest way to perform a search for matching messages is to type search text into the search box. See **Table 7.1** for some examples.

To perform a basic search:

1. Type search text into the search box (**Figure 7.2**) by doing one of the following:
   - ▲ Enter a single word to search for messages that contain the word.
   - ▲ Enter multiple words to perform a search in which *both* words are present in the message (although not necessarily together).
   - ▲ Enter multiple words surrounded by quotation marks to perform a search in which *both* words are present in the message and together.
   - ▲ Enter multiple words separated by *OR* (in capital letters) to perform a search in which at least *one* of the words is present in the message.
2. Click Search Mail.

   Matching messages and conversations are displayed in a list (**Figure 7.3**).

continues on next page

Table 7.1

Basic Search Examples*

Example	Explanation
baseball	Find messages that contain the word *baseball* in the message body or Subject
baseball picture	Find messages that contain the words *baseball* and *picture* in the message body or Subject, but not necessarily together
"baseball picture"	Find the specific text string *baseball picture* in the message body or Subject; the words must be together
baseball OR picture	Find messages that contain the word *baseball* or *picture* in the message body or Subject
Steve	Find all messages to/from Steve (as part of the contact name, user name, or in the message)
aol	Find all messages from people who are America Online (aol.com) subscribers

*Quoted strings and OR searches rely on advanced search operators, as discussed in Appendix B. They are included here because such searches are commonplace.

3. *Do any of the following:*
   - ▲ Read any found message or conversation by clicking its header. Matching text is highlighted.
   - ▲ Click check boxes of certain headers and select an action from the More Actions drop-down list.
4. After opening a found message or conversation, you can return to the list by clicking Back to Search results (**Figure 7.4**).

   Or if you're finished with this search, click any of the section links on the left side of the page.

✔ Tips

- A basic search checks for matching text in all parts of a message, including the Subject and the email addresses of all senders and recipients.
- Basic searches do not include messages stored in Spam or Trash.
- Search text isn't case sensitive. You could enter *mexico* or *Mexico*, for example.
- Searches will not find partial strings. Searching for *airplane* will not find *airplanes*, for example.
- When searching for an email address, partial searches *are* allowed. You can search for a user name (*Kevin777*) or the domain (*redriver.net*).
- Searches are now more flexible when searching for attachments by file type. For example, searching for *tif* or *TIFF* will find all TIFF graphic files; searching for *jpg* or *JPEG* will find all JPEG files.
- You can enable or disable the yellow match highlighting by clicking a text link to the right of the open message or conversation (**Figure 7.5**).

Figure 7.4 To examine other found messages or conversations, click Back to Search results.

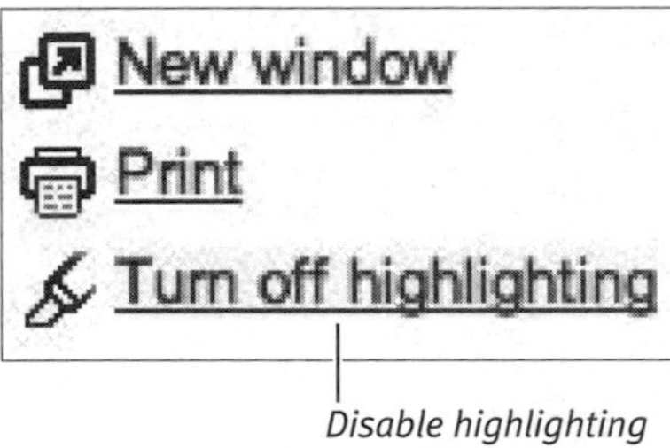

Figure 7.5 You can turn match highlighting off or on by clicking this link.

Performing an Advanced Search

Using Gmail's advanced search features, you can set more specific search criteria. There are two ways to perform an advanced search. You can open the Search Options pane, or you can include advanced search operators in the search text.

To perform an advanced search using the Search Options pane:

1. Click Show search options (see Figure 7.1).

   The Search Options pane appears (**Figure 7.6**).

2. *Do one of the following:*
   - ▲ To find messages and conversations that match a criterion, enter text in a box, click the Has attachment check box, or specify a date range.
   - ▲ To find messages and conversations that match multiple criteria (an AND search), specify as many criteria as you like.

continues on next page

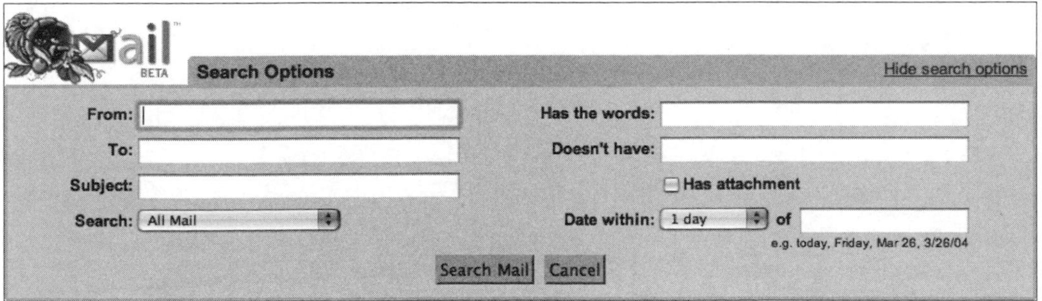

Figure 7.6 Enter search criteria and click the Search Mail button.

3. *Optional:* From the Search drop-down list (**Figure 7.7**), select the Gmail section(s) to search.
4. Click Search Mail.

   Matching messages and conversations are displayed in a list (see Figure 7.3).

✔ Tips

- If you decide that you'd rather perform a basic search, click Hide search options (see Figure 7.6).
- In the From or To box, you can enter a person's complete name or email address, only the person's first or last name, or only the user name or domain from the person's email address.
- The Has the words and Doesn't have criteria are normally used together. Enter a word or words in the Doesn't have box to select messages and conversations that do *not* contain the word(s).
- You can only search for messages in Spam and Trash by performing an advanced search. From the Search drop-down list (see Figure 7.7), select Spam, Trash, or All & Spam & Trash.

Figure 7.7 You can restrict a search to a specific Gmail section, read or unread mail, or a label.

Figure 7.8 In this search, only messages with the word *picture* in the Subject line will be identified.

To perform a search using advanced search operators:

1. In the search box, include advanced search operators in the search text (**Figure 7.8**).

   See Appendix B for the list of operators and examples of how to use them.

2. Click Search Mail.

   Matching messages and conversations are displayed in a list (see Figure 7.3).

Conducting a Web Search

You can also use the search box to perform a Google Web search.

To perform a Google search:

- Enter search text in the search box (**Figure 7.9**), and click Search the Web.

  A new browser window opens and displays the search results (**Figure 7.10**).

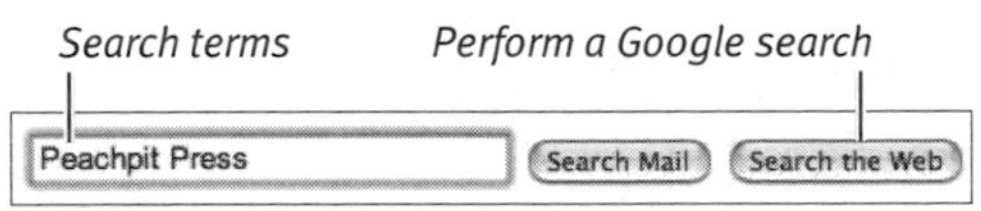

Figure 7.9 Enter search terms and then click Search the Web.

Perform an advanced search

Peachpit Press – Google Search

http://www.google.com/search?sourceid=gmail&q=Peachpit%20Pr

Apple (176) Amazon eBay Yahoo! News (963) Personals Hotmail Gmail Netflix ANYwebcam

lizAZ@gmail.com | My Account | Sign out

Web Images Groups News Froogle LocalNew! more »

Google Peachpit Press Search Advanced Search Preferences

Web Results **1** - **10** of about **2,410,000** for **Peachpit Press**. (**0.18** seconds)

Peachpit Press
Specialize in graphics, web design and development, and digital imaging books with a searchable index of authors, books and subjects.
www.**peachpit**.com/ - 20k - Nov 27, 2005 - Cached - Similar pages
Bookstore - Series
Stylin' with CSS: A Designer's Guide - $... - Articles
More results from www.peachpit.com »

Pearson Education - **Peachpit Press**
Peachpit Press specialises in the area of web development. ... **Peachpit Press** is
the home of the internationally recognized Visual QuickStart Guide series, ...
www.pearsoned.co.uk/Imprints/PeachpitPress/ - 21k - Nov 27, 2005 - Cached - Similar pages

Cookwood **Press** - Elizabeth Castro
Her books are published by **Peachpit Press**, the leading publisher of web and design books, based in Berkeley, California. Elizabeth's newest book is a guide ...
www.cookwood.com/ - 5k - Cached - Similar pages

Amazon.com Books: **Peachpit Press**
Peachpit Press spoke with Michael Wohl, author of Editing Techniques with ...
Peachpit Press interviewed Michael Rubin, author of The Little Digital Video ...
www.amazon.com/exec/obidos/tg/browse/-/764450 - 37k - Cached - Similar pages

Peachpit Press Home on creativepro.com
Online Store: http://www.**peachpit**.com/books/index.html Sales: 800-283-9444
510-524-2178 http://www.**peachpit**.com/order/index.html Web Site: ...
www.creativepro.com/company/home/69.html - 27k - Nov 27, 2005 - Cached - Similar pages

Peachpit Press
The **Peachpit Press** Book List (Published books can be purchased through the WWWiz Bookstore. ... (Available Dec 1997), **Peachpit Press**, $19. Talitha Harper & ...
wwwiz.com/books/**peachpit**.html - 10k - Cached - Similar pages

Sponsored Links

Computer Product Prices
42,600+ Computer Product Products
Read User Reviews!
www.NexTag.com/ComputerProducts

Peachpit Press Books
Academic Superstore has Low Pricing on **Peachpit Press** Books and More.
www.AcademicSuperstore.com

Figure 7.10 Google's site opens in a new window and shows the results of your search.

✔ Tips

- Capitalization is ignored during a search.
- To search for a specific phrase, enclose it in quotation marks. This technique is especially useful when searching for people, song titles, lyrics, and famous quotes.
- To exclude a term from a search, precede it with a minus (-). To find monarch butterflies but not the car model of the same name, you might enter the following:

  `monarch butterfly -car`
- To specify a word that *must* appear in the results, precede it with a plus (+).
- To perform an advanced search, click the Advanced Search link beside Google's Search button (see Figure 7.10). You can then create your search criteria by typing terms and selecting options from drop-down lists (**Figure 7.11**).

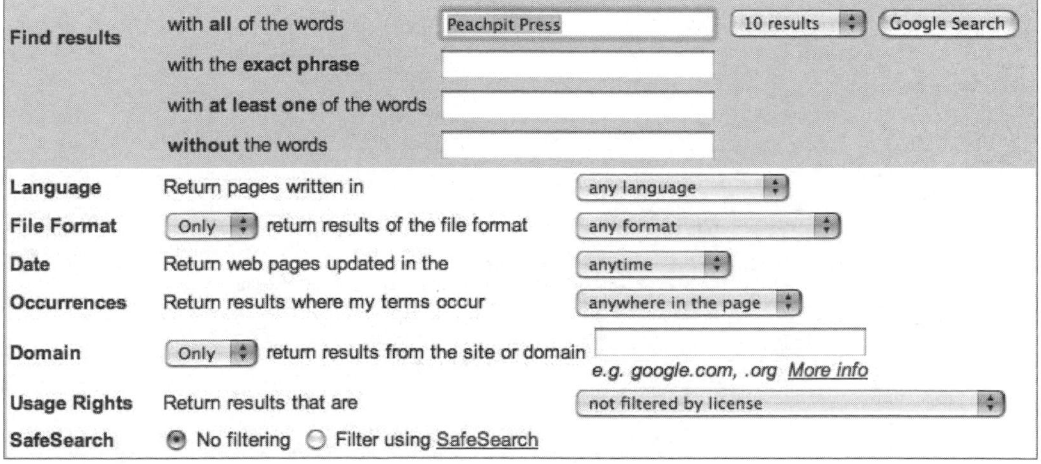

Figure 7.11 Rather than typing search terms into a single box, you can create more complex searches on the Advanced Search page.

Using Filters

You can create filters to select certain incoming messages and automatically perform actions on them. A maximum of 20 filters can be defined. Filter actions can include any combination of the following:

- Bypassing the Inbox, archiving the message to All Mail
- Applying a star to the message
- Assigning a label to the message
- Forwarding the message to another email address
- Placing the message in the Trash

To create a filter:

1. At the top of any Gmail page, click the Create a filter link.

   The Create a Filter pane (**Figure 7.12**) appears at the top of the page.

2. Enter filter criteria in the boxes.

   You can specify a single criterion (such as *Hammond* in the From box or *poker* in the Subject box), or enter multiple criteria for more complex selection requirements.

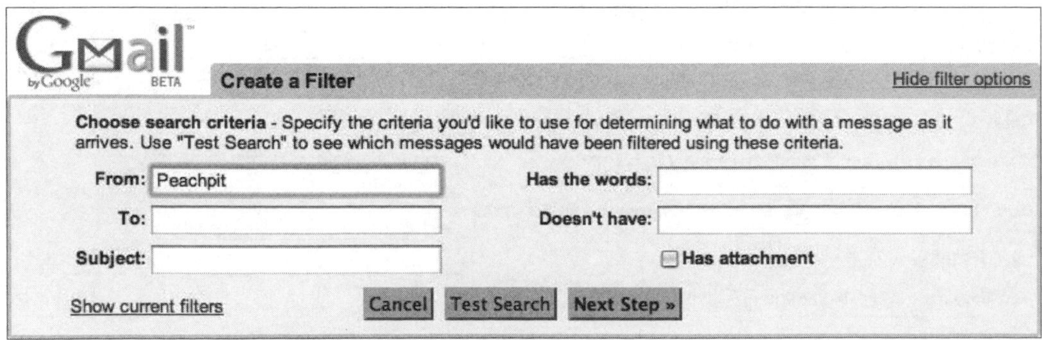

Figure 7.12 Specify the filter criteria in this section of the Create a Filter pane.

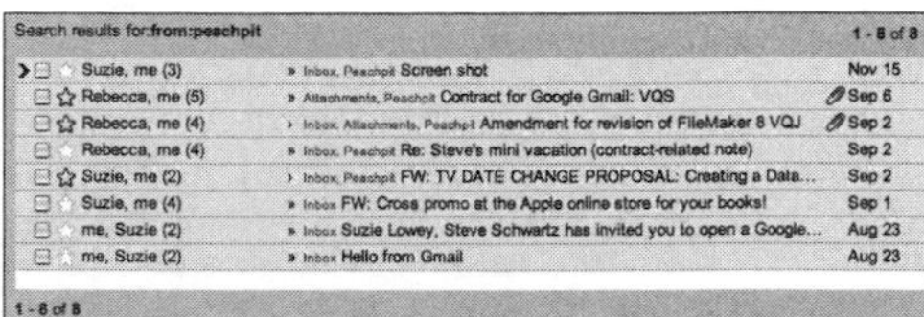

Figure 7.13 These messages are selected by the filter criterion *From:Peachpit*.

3. *Optional:* Click Test Search to test the selection criteria on your existing messages.

   The selected messages appear in a Search results list below the Create a Filter pane (**Figure 7.13**).

4. Click the Next Step button.

   The Choose action options are displayed (**Figure 7.14**).

5. Specify the filter's actions.

   A filter can perform one or multiple actions on the selected messages.

6. Click the Create Filter button.

   The new filter is added to the list on the Filters tab of the Settings page.

✔ Tips

- To specify multiple email addresses as From criteria, separate addresses with an *OR* and surround the entire group with parentheses.
- You can create a filter to make it simple to find all messages with attachments. Click the Has attachment check box as the sole criterion (see Figure 7.12). Then apply a label named Attachments.
- Using the Forward it to filter action, you can forward critical email to another account, such as your primary email address or a business account. Just click the Forward it to check box and enter a complete email address in the text box.

Using Filters

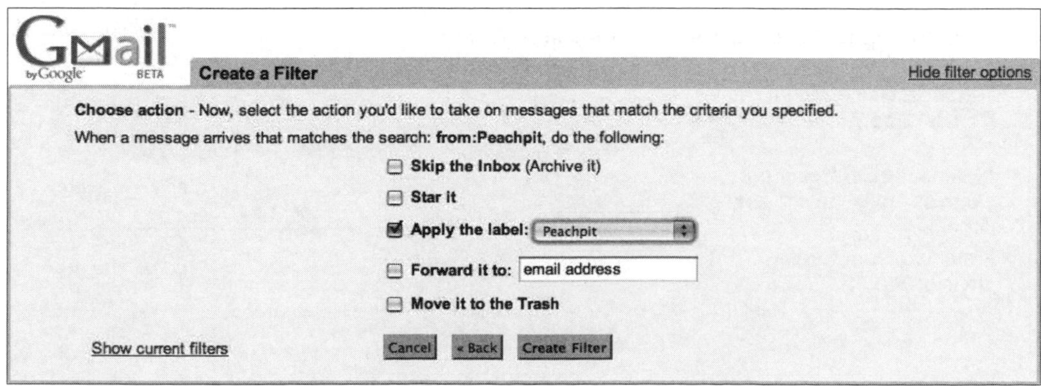

Figure 7.14 Specify the actions that will be performed on messages selected by the filter.

To edit or delete a filter:

1. Click the Settings link at the top of any Gmail page. On the Mail Settings page, click the Filters link.

   The list of defined filters is shown (**Figure 7.15**).

2. *Do one of the following:*
   - ▲ To delete a filter, click the delete link to the right of the filter's name.
   - ▲ To edit a filter, click the edit link to the right of the filter's name. The Create a Filter pane appears (see Figure 7.12) with the original criteria displayed. Make any desired changes, performing Steps 2–6 from the previous step list.

✔ Tip

- When you delete a filter, no confirmation dialog box appears; filter deletions are irreversible.

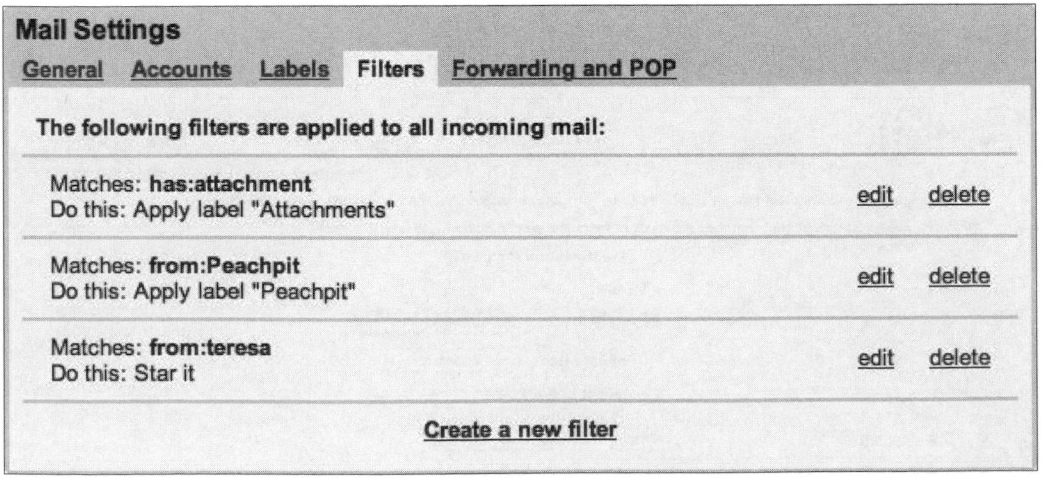

Mail Settings

General Accounts Labels **Filters** Forwarding and POP

The following filters are applied to all incoming mail:

Matches: **has:attachment**
Do this: Apply label "Attachments" edit delete

Matches: **from:Peachpit**
Do this: Apply label "Peachpit" edit delete

Matches: **from:teresa**
Do this: Star it edit delete

Create a new filter

Figure 7.15 To review, edit, or delete filters, go to the Filters tab of Mail Settings.

8

GMAIL AND POP

Accessing Gmail from a Web browser is simple and easy, but it isn't always convenient. For instance, it *requires* you to have an active Internet connection—even when all you want to do is review or print old messages.

Because Gmail also has *POP3* (Post Office Protocol) mail servers, there are two simple solutions to this problem that are described in this chapter:

- You can use *POP forwarding* to forward copies of all or selected incoming messages to an existing email account, such as one provided by your *ISP* (Internet Service Provider) or company.
- You can enable *POP access* in Gmail, and then create a Gmail account in your regular email program, such as Outlook Express or Entourage. Doing so will let you send and receive Gmail directly from your email program.

Enabling POP Forwarding

The *POP forwarding* option causes Gmail to email a copy of every new incoming message to another email account. If you normally keep an email program running, this allows you to instantly receive new Gmail messages without having to launch your Web browser.

To enable POP forwarding:

1. In Gmail, click the Settings link at the top of any page.

   The Mail Settings page appears.

2. Click the Forwarding and POP link (**Figure 8.1**).

3. In the Forwarding section, click Forward a copy of incoming mail to and type the destination email address in the text box.

   Enter a *complete* email address in the box in the form *username@domain*, such as roadrunner17@cablepro.net.

4. Select one of the following mail-handling options from the pop-up list:
   - ▲ *keep Gmail's copy in the Inbox.* This is the default option. When selected, Gmail's message lists are unaffected.
   - ▲ *archive Gmail's copy.* When selected, forwarded email is removed from Gmail's Inbox and archived to the All Mail section.
   - ▲ *trash Gmail's copy.* When selected, after forwarding a new message to the designated account, Gmail moves the message from the Inbox to the Trash.

5. Click Save Changes.

✔ Tip

- Messages in the Trash (**Figure 8.2**) can be read until they are manually deleted (by clicking Delete Forever) or automatically deleted (30 days after being placed in the Trash).

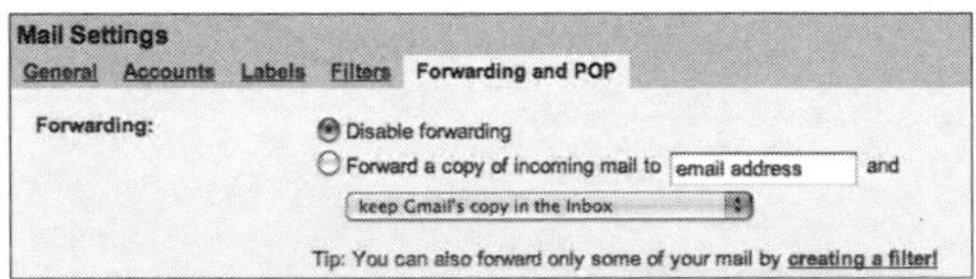

Figure 8.1 You can enable POP forwarding and specify a target email account on the Mail Settings page.

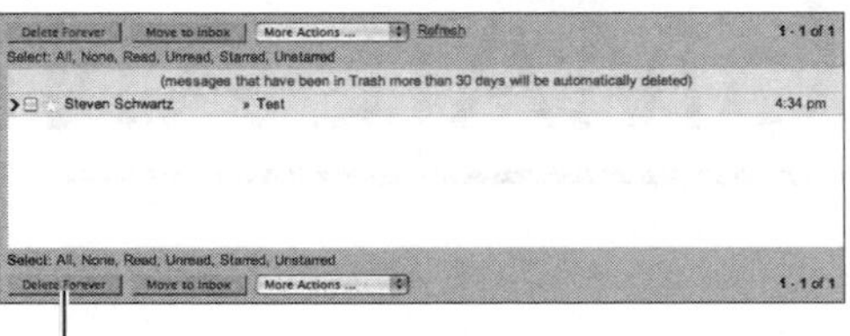

Figure 8.2 To permanently delete a message in the Trash, select it by clicking its check box, and then click Delete Forever.

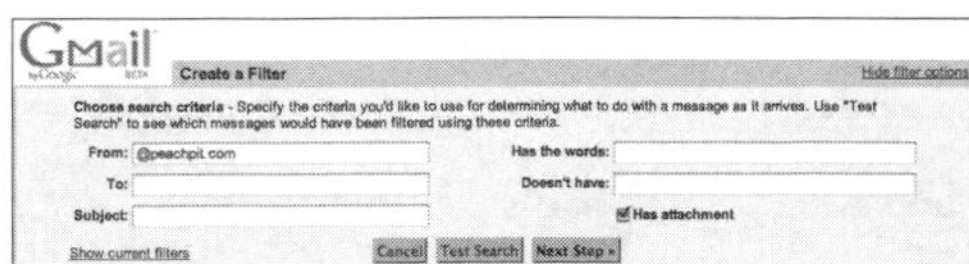

Figure 8.3 Enter criteria that will be used to select the messages to forward.

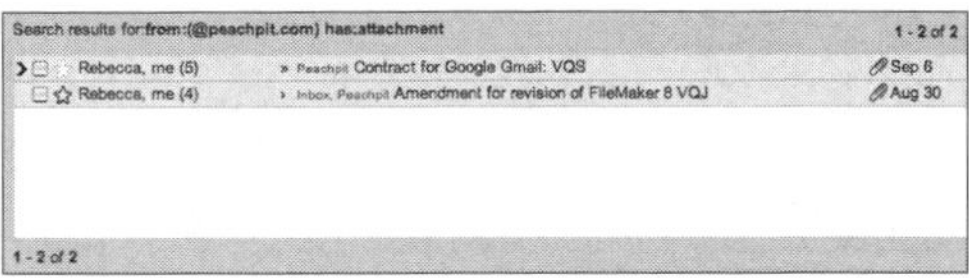

Figure 8.4 If you have existing email that should be selected by this filter, you can test it and examine the results.

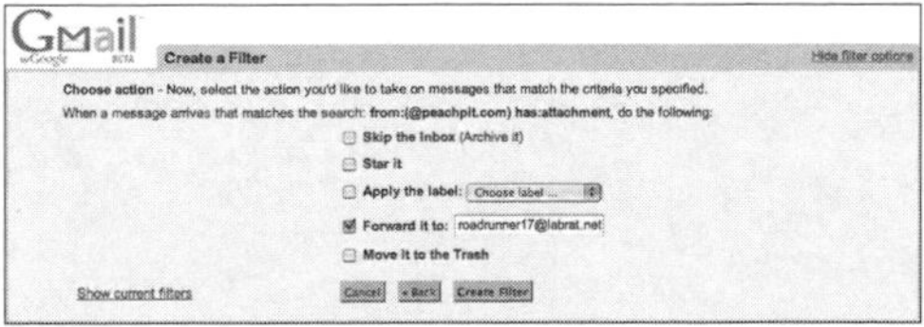

Figure 8.5 Enter criteria that will be used to select the messages to forward.

To forward only certain messages:

1. Optionally, you can restrict forwarded messages to those that match a filter's criteria. Begin by clicking the Create a filter link at the top of any page.

   The Create a Filter section opens at the top of the Web page (**Figure 8.3**).

2. Enter the criteria that will be used to select messages for forwarding. (You can set multiple criteria, but only messages that satisfy *all* criteria will be forwarded.)

   For example, to forward only mail from my contacts at Peachpit Press, I could enter *@peachpit.com* in the From box. Or to forward only one person's messages, I could enter his or her email address.

3. *Optional:* Click Test Search to apply the filter to your current Gmail messages.

   The results (**Figure 8.4**) appear beneath the filter criteria. If the desired messages are found, click Next Step. Otherwise, refine the criteria and repeat this step.

4. Click the Forward it to: check box (**Figure 8.5**), and enter the email address to which messages should be forwarded.

   If desired, you can set other message handling options, such as moving the original message to the Trash.

5. Click the Create Filter button.

   The filter is created and added to your filters list.

✔ Tip

- To modify this filter or delete it (when selective forwarding is no longer desired, for example), click the Settings link on any page and then click the Filters link.

Enabling POP Access

When POP access is enabled, you can send and receive Gmail messages using your regular email program (**Figure 8.6**), such as Microsoft Outlook, Outlook Express, or Entourage. There are advantages to configuring Gmail to allow POP access:

- You'll have a permanent copy of all Gmail messages that you can view and print without having to be online. (All POP messages are stored on your computer.)
- You can take advantage of your email program's special features, such as creating new storage folders, compressing file attachments, and junk mail filtering.

The only disadvantage of enabling POP access is that you lose Gmail's features, such as threaded conversations and message filtering. Note, however, that with POP access enabled, you can continue to use Gmail with any Web browser.

There are two steps to perform before you can send and receive Gmail from an email program. First, you must enable POP access in Gmail. Second, you must create a Gmail account in your email program.

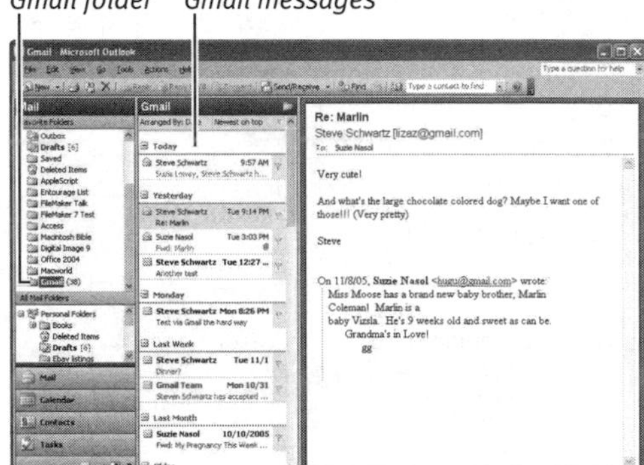

Figure 8.6 When POP access is enabled, you can send and receive Gmail messages using your favorite email client, such as Microsoft Office Outlook 2003.

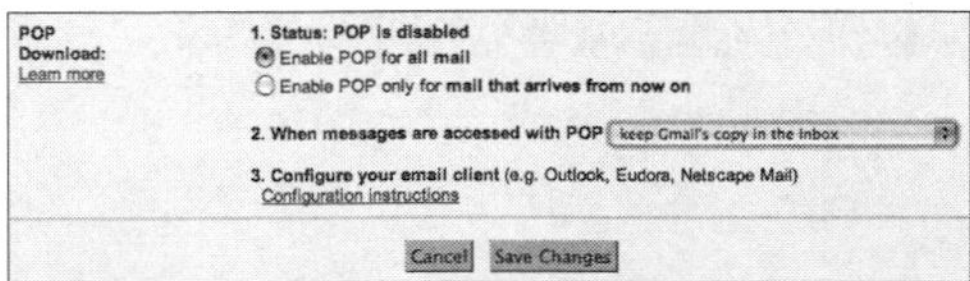

Figure 8.7 POP access can be enabled or disabled on the Mail Settings page.

To enable POP access:

1. In Gmail, click the Settings link at the top of any page.

   The Mail Settings page appears.

2. Click the Forwarding and POP link (see Figure 8.1).

3. In the POP Download section (**Figure 8.7**), select one of the following options:

   - *Enable POP for all mail.* Select this option if you want to download a copy of *every* Gmail message that currently exists, as well as new messages that arrive or are created in the future.
   - *Enable POP only for mail that arrives from now on.* Select this option to download only new Gmail messages that arrive or are created.

4. Select an option from the When messages are accessed with POP pop-up list:

   - *keep Gmail's copy in the Inbox.* This is the default option. When selected, Gmail's message lists are unaffected.
   - *archive Gmail's copy.* When selected, messages that you download to your POP account are removed from Gmail's Inbox and archived to the All Mail section.
   - *trash Gmail's copy.* When selected, messages that you download to your POP account are moved from Gmail's Inbox to the Trash.

5. Click Save Changes.

6. Create a Gmail account in your email program. Doing so will enable you to create and receive Gmail messages in the email program. Outgoing messages from this account will be treated as though they were sent from your Gmail address.

   See the following pages for instructions on configuring popular email clients.

Configuring Email Clients

After enabling POP access, the next step is to configure your email program to send and receive mail using Gmail's POP3 mail servers. You do this by creating a new account.

The following instructions show you how to configure several popular Windows and Mac email programs to access Gmail. If your program isn't listed, you'll note that while the setup procedure varies from one program to the next, the specific *settings* do not.

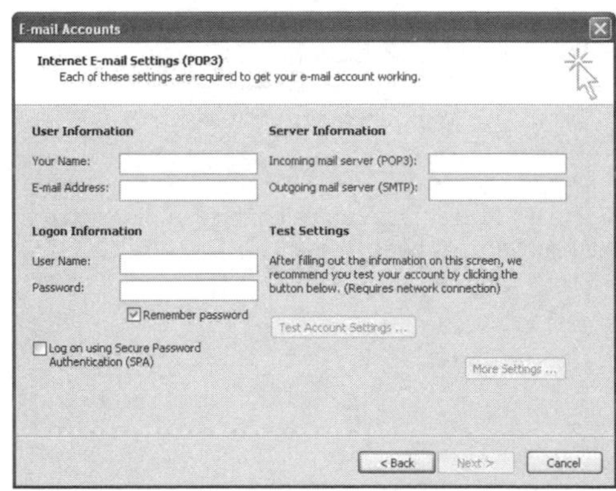

Figure 8.8 Most of the important POP settings for your Gmail account are entered on this wizard screen.

To configure Microsoft Office Outlook 2003 (Windows):

1. In Outlook 2003, choose Tools > E-mail Accounts.

   The E-mail Accounts wizard appears.

2. Select Add a new e-mail account and click Next.

3. On the Server Type screen, select POP3 and click Next.

   The Internet E-mail Settings (POP3) screen appears (**Figure 8.8**).

4. *Enter the following information:*
   - ▲ **Your Name:** Enter the name that will identify you to message recipients.
   - ▲ **Email Address:** Enter your complete Gmail email address.
   - ▲ **Incoming mail server:** pop.gmail.com
   - ▲ **Outgoing mail server:** smtp.gmail.com
   - ▲ **User Name:** Enter your complete Gmail email address.
   - ▲ **Password**: Enter your Gmail log-in password.

5. Click the More Settings button.

   The Internet E-Mail Settings dialog box appears.

Preparing for the First Download

While you're setting up a Gmail account in your email client, you generally need to be online so the account settings can be tested. However, *after* creating the account, you'll want to quickly go offline. (Microsoft programs make this easy. Choose the Work Offline command.)

The reason you shouldn't immediately download Gmail into your email program is because few email programs provide a separate mail folder for each new account. To prevent your Gmail from downloading into the Inbox (along with all non-Gmail account messages), you'll want to make a separate folder for Gmail, as well as create a message rule or filter that automatically files Gmail messages in the new folder. (Instructions for creating a message rule for Outlook 2003 are provided on the next page.)

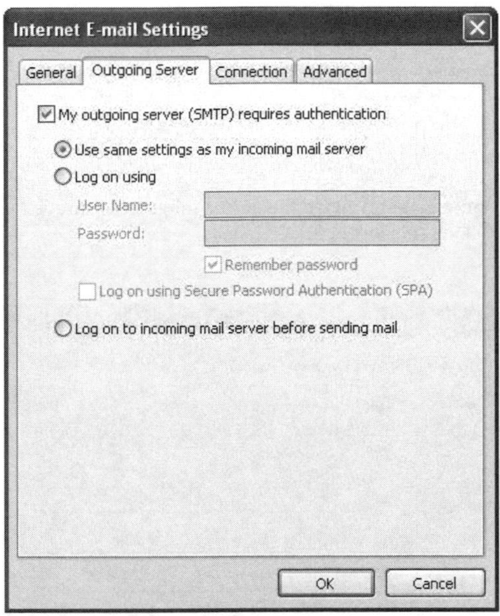

Figure 8.9 Outgoing Server settings.

Internet E-mail Settings
General | Outgoing Server | Connection | Advanced
Server Port Numbers
Incoming server (POP3): 995 Use Defaults
This server requires an encrypted connection (SSL)
Outgoing server (SMTP): 465
This server requires an encrypted connection (SSL)
Server Timeouts
Short Long 1 minute
Delivery
Leave a copy of messages on the server
Remove from server after 10 days
Remove from server when deleted from 'Deleted Items'
OK Cancel

Figure 8.10 Advanced settings.

6. On the General tab, enter a descriptive name for the account (Gmail, for example) in the Mail Account box.
7. On the Outgoing Server tab (**Figure 8.9**), click My outgoing server (SMTP) requires authentication. Select Use same settings as my incoming mail server.
8. On the Advanced tab (**Figure 8.10**), click the check boxes in the Incoming server and Outgoing server sections. Set the Outgoing server port to 465.
9. Click OK to dismiss the dialog box and return to the E-mail Accounts wizard.
10. Click the Test Account Settings button.

    Outlook contacts Gmail's POP servers and performs a test send/receive.
11. Close the test window, click Next, and click Finish.

✔ Tips

- Prior to your first Gmail send/receive in Outlook 2003, create a new Outlook folder (Gmail) in which to store your messages. Then choose Tools > Rules and Alerts, and create this *message rule* to automatically route incoming Gmail messages to the Gmail folder:

```
Apply this rule after the message arrives
through the Gmail account
   and on this machine only
move it to the Gmail folder
```

- You can create a send/receive schedule to periodically check for new Gmail messages. Choose Tools > Send/Receive > Send/Receive Settings > Define Send/Receive Groups (Ctrl Alt S).

To configure Outlook Express 6, Microsoft Outlook 2002, and earlier versions (Windows):

1. Gmail provides an *auto-configuration tool* that can set up Gmail POP access for you. On the Forwarding and Pop tab of the Mail Settings page, click the Configuration instructions link near the bottom of the page (see Figure 8.7).

   A Gmail Help page opens.
2. Click the Outlook Express and Outlook 2002 (Windows) link.

   A new Help page appears.
3. Click Run the auto-configuration tool (**Figure 8.11**).
4. In the File Download dialog box that appears (**Figure 8.12**), click Run.
5. After the utility downloads to your computer, a new dialog box appears asking: "Do you want to run this software?" Click the Run button.

   The Gmail Client Configuration Setup utility launches (**Figure 8.13**).
6. Select the email client to configure. In the text boxes, enter your Gmail user name and the name that will identify you to message recipients. Click the Configure button.
7. The utility configures the specified email program and displays a new dialog box. Click Finish.

✔ Tips

- You can change the resulting settings. For example, your password can automatically be supplied when checking for new Gmail, rather than requesting it each time. In Outlook Express, choose Tools > Accounts. In the Internet Accounts dialog box, select the Gmail account and click Properties.

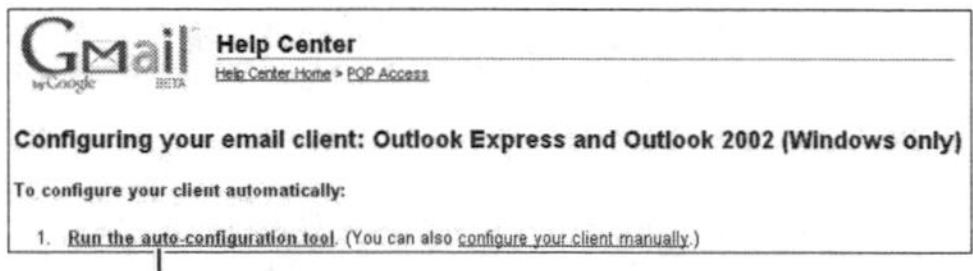

Figure 8.11 Download the auto-configuration tool by clicking this link in Gmail Help.

Figure 8.12 Click the Run button to download the auto-configuration tool.

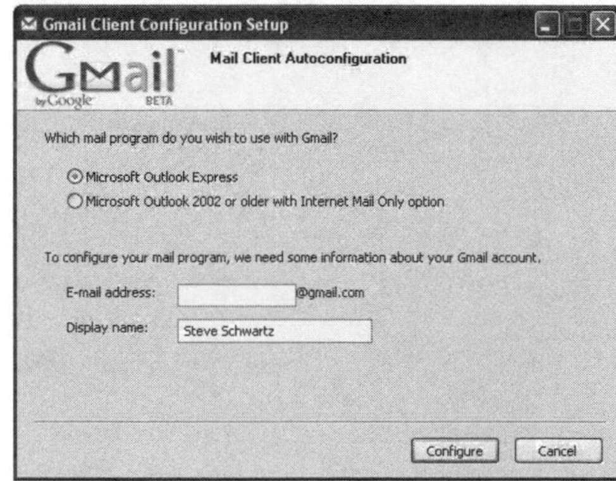

Figure 8.13 Select an email program, enter the requested information, and click Configure.

- Outlook Express and Microsoft Outlook can also be configured *manually*. See Gmail Help for instructions.

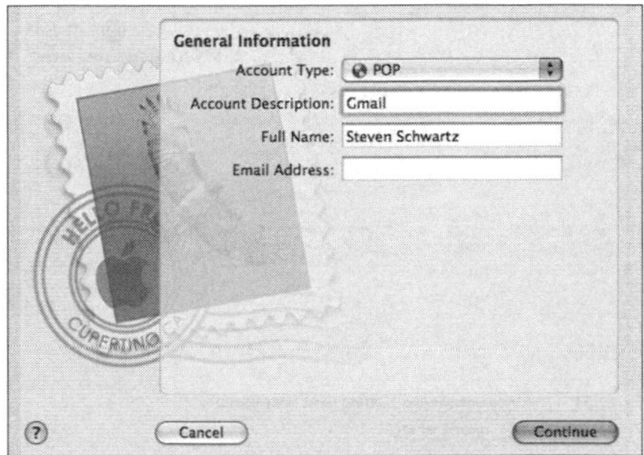

Figure 8.14 The General Information screen.

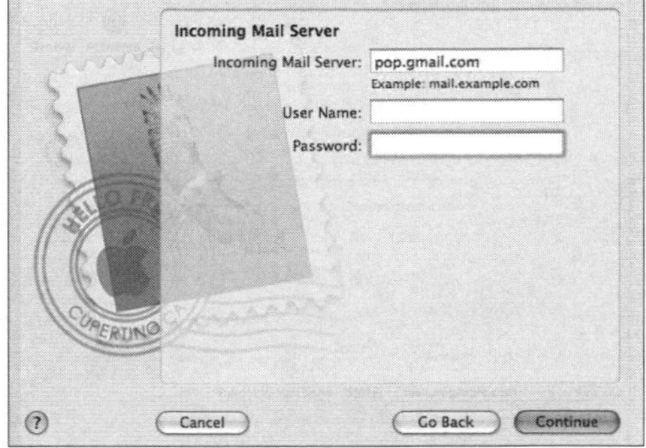

Figure 8.15 The Incoming Mail Server screen.

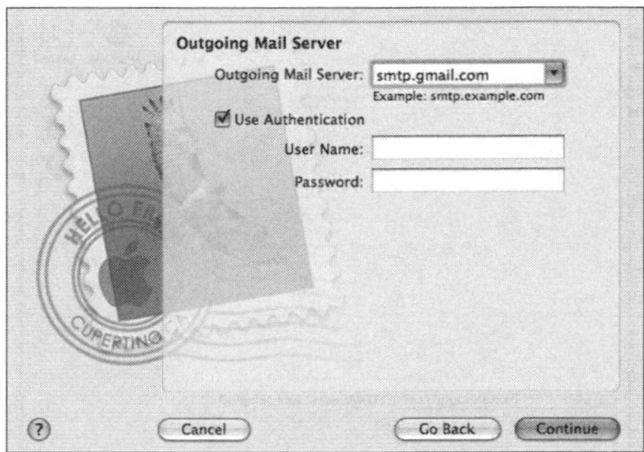

Figure 8.16 The Outgoing Mail Server screen.

To configure Apple Mail 2.0 (Mac OS X):

1. In Apple Mail, choose Mail > Preferences.
2. Click the Accounts icon at the top of the dialog box that appears. Then click the plus (+) icon at the bottom to create a new email account.
3. On the General Information screen (**Figure 8.14**), select/enter the following:
   - ▲ **Account Type:** POP
   - ▲ **Account Description:** any identifier, such as Gmail
   - ▲ **Full Name:** your name as you want it to appear on sent Gmail messages
   - ▲ **Email Address:** your full Gmail email address (*username*@gmail.com)

   Click Continue.
4. On the Incoming Mail Server screen (**Figure 8.15**), enter the following:
   - ▲ **Incoming Server:** pop.gmail.com
   - ▲ **User Name:** your full Gmail email address (*username*@gmail.com)
   - ▲ **Password:** Gmail log-in password

   Click Continue.
5. On the Outgoing Mail Server screen (**Figure 8.16**), enter the following:
   - ▲ **Outgoing Server:** smtp.gmail.com
   - ▲ **Use Authentication:** checked
   - ▲ **User Name:** your full Gmail email address (*username*@gmail.com)
   - ▲ **Password:** Gmail log-in password

   Click Continue, and then click Done. The Accounts dialog box reappears. (If you click the Advanced tab, you'll see that the port has been set to 995.)
6. Close the Accounts dialog box.

To configure Microsoft Entourage 2004 (Mac OS X):

1. In Entourage 2004 (a component of Microsoft Office 2004), choose Tools > Accounts.
2. In the Accounts dialog box, select the Mail tab and click New.

   Either the New Account or the Set Up a Mail Account dialog box appears. If the latter, click Configure account manually.
3. In the New Account dialog box (**Figure 8.17**), select POP as the Account type, and then click OK.

   The Edit Account dialog box appears (**Figure 8.18**).
4. *Enter the following information:*
   - **Account name:** any identifier, such as Gmail
   - **Name:** your name as you want it to appear on sent Gmail messages
   - **E-mail address:** your Gmail address
   - **Account ID:** your Gmail address
   - **POP server:** pop.gmail.com
   - **Password:** Gmail log-in password
   - **SMTP server:** smtp.gmail.com
5. *Optional:* To instruct Entourage to remember your password rather than prompting for it, click Save password in my Mac OS keychain.

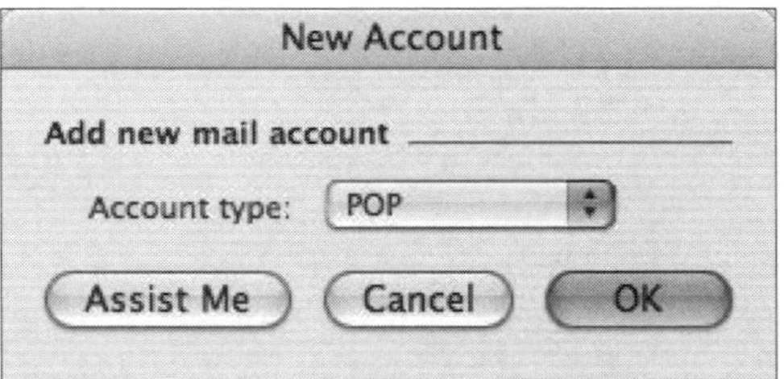

Figure 8.17 Select POP as the Account type.

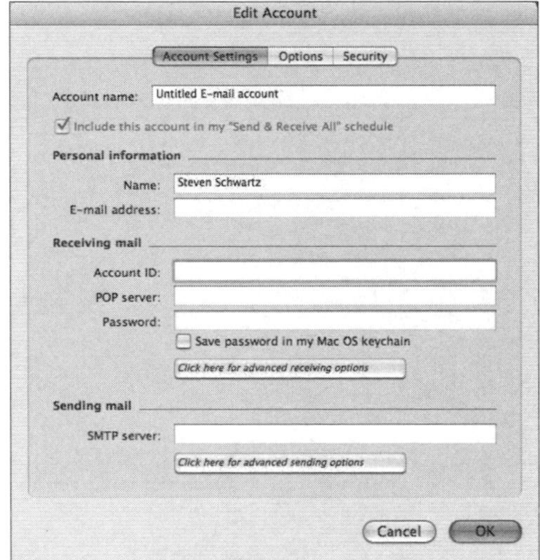

Figure 8.18 The Edit Account dialog box.

Figure 8.19 Set advanced receiving options to match the ones shown here.

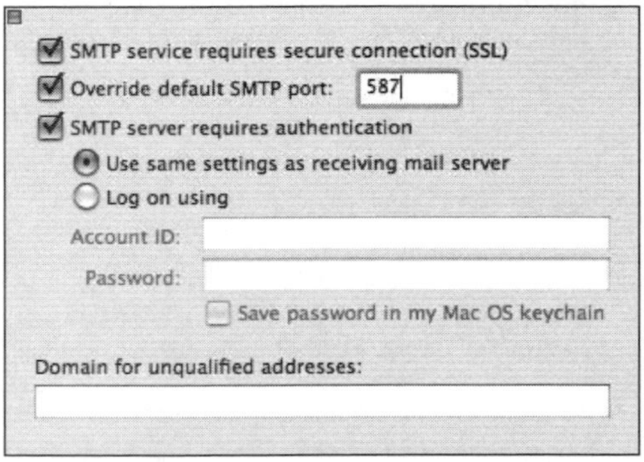

Figure 8.20 Set advanced sending options to match the ones shown here.

Configuring Other Email Clients

To configure an email program not covered in this chapter, see Gmail Help for instructions or enter these settings:

- **Incoming Mail (POP3) Server:** pop.gmail.com; use SSL; port 995
- **Outgoing Mail (SMTP) Server:** smtp.gmail.com; use authentication
- **TLS:** use authentication; use STARTTLS (or SSL); port 465 or 587
- **Account Name, User Name:** Enter your complete Gmail email address.
- **Password:** Enter your Gmail log-in password.

6. Click the Click here for advanced receiving options button.

   A windoid (**Figure 8.19**) pops up.

7. Click This POP service requires a secure connection (SSL).

   To close the windoid, click its close box or anywhere in the Edit Account dialog box.

8. Click the Click here for advanced sending options button.

   A windoid (**Figure 8.20**) pops up.

9. Click the three check boxes at the top of the windoid, and enter 587 as the SMTP port.

   To close the windoid, click its close box or anywhere in the Edit Account dialog box.

10. To save the settings for the new account, click OK to close the Edit Account dialog box.

    The new account name appears in the Accounts dialog box.

Creating a Gmail folder and rule

Before downloading your Gmail messages into Entourage, you may also want to perform the following steps. Doing so will prevent your Gmail from being commingled with the Inbox messages.

To automatically store Gmail in its own folder:

1. With the Mail icon and the Inbox folder selected, choose File > New > Folder. An untitled folder appears in the folders list; change its name to Gmail.
2. To create a rule to automatically file Gmail messages in the new Gmail folder, choose Tools > Rules.

   The Rules dialog box appears.
3. Ensure that the Mail (POP) tab is selected and click New.

   The Edit Rule dialog box appears.
4. Match the settings shown in **Figure 8.21**. (Set the criterion to Account is *gmail account*. Set the action to Move message to the Gmail folder.)
5. Click OK. Then close the Rules dialog box.

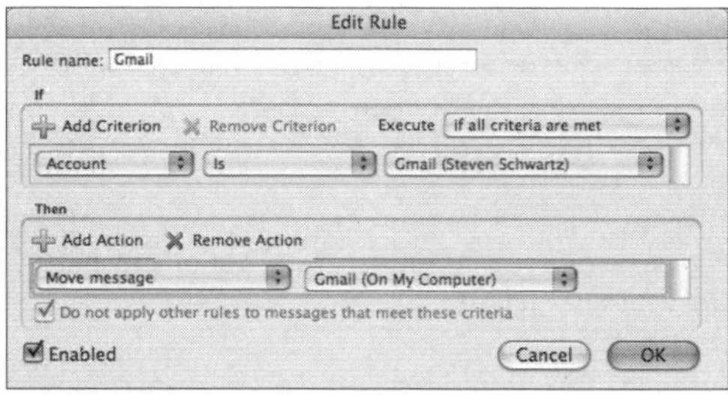

Figure 8.21 When enabled, this message rule will automatically place all Gmail messages in the Gmail folder.

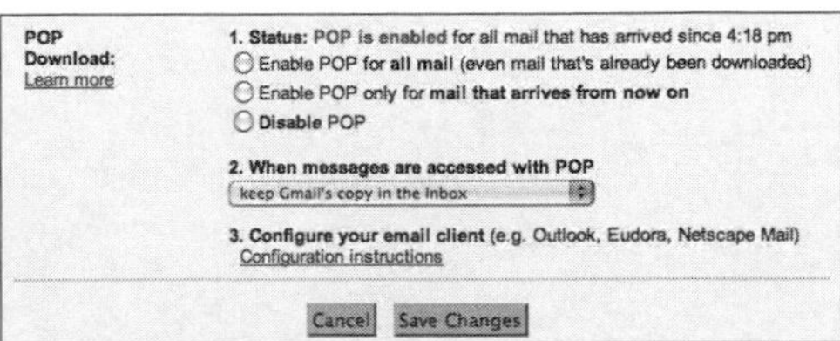

Figure 8.22 After initially enabling POP access, the POP Download options change to allow you to download all Gmail additional times.

Recovering from download problems

Unfortunately, there are things that can go wrong the first time you download Gmail into your email client:

- All messages may be downloaded into your Inbox, commingled with messages from your other email accounts.
- You've configured more than one email program (perhaps on multiple machines), but only the first program receives your entire Gmail message list. The second and subsequent programs/computers only receive *new* Gmail messages.

To recover from an error in the initial download:

- *Do any of the following:*
  - In your email program, create a folder for your Gmail and manually move the downloaded messages into this folder.
  - If your email client supports message rules, create a rule to automatically store retrieved Gmail messages in their own folder. (You may be able to apply this rule to the previously downloaded Gmail messages, moving them from the Inbox into the proper folder.)
  - To download your Gmail again (to another email client or to the original client after deleting all messages from the first attempt), go to the Forwarding and Pop tab of the Mail Settings page. In the POP Download section (**Figure 8.22**), select Enable POP for all mail (even mail that's already been downloaded), and click Save Changes.

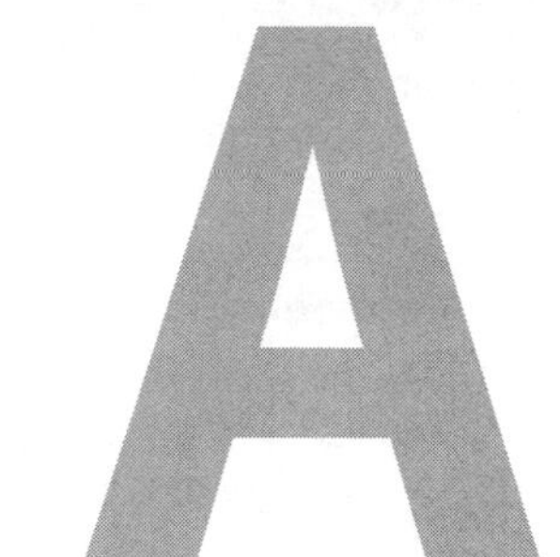

Keystroke Reference

When *keyboard shortcuts* are enabled, Gmail watches for certain keystrokes and then performs a particular action. To enable or disable keyboard shortcuts, click the Settings link at the top of any Gmail page, select Keyboard shortcuts on or Keyboard shortcuts off (**Figure A.1**), and then click Save Changes.

Keyboard shortcuts:
Learn more
○ Keyboard shortcuts off
◉ Keyboard shortcuts on

Figure A.1 Visit the Settings page (General tab) to enable or disable keyboard shortcuts.

The tables in this appendix explain the Gmail keyboard shortcuts. Note that keyboard shortcuts are available in Standard View, but *not* in Basic HTML View.

✔ Tip

- Shortcuts work better in some browsers than in others. For example, Safari 2.0 (Macintosh) sometimes responds to shortcuts and sometimes doesn't.

Table A.1

Go to List Commands	
KEYSTROKE(S)	TASK
g a	Go to All Mail
g c	Go to Contacts
g d	Go to Drafts
g i	Go to Inbox
g s	Go to Starred

Table A.2

Conversation Commands†	
KEYSTROKE(S)	TASK
o or Enter	When viewing a conversation list, open the selected conversation; when reading a conversation, expand or collapse the current message
n	Go to next message in the current conversation
p	Go to previous message in the current conversation
k	Go to the next newer conversation
j	Go to the next older conversation
s	Apply or remove a star from the current conversation
x	Select or deselect the current conversation (by clicking its check box)
y	When viewing an Inbox conversation, archive the conversation; in Starred, remove the star; in Trash, move to Inbox; from a label, remove the label
u	Return to the conversation list (when viewing a conversation)

†Many of these shortcuts can be used when reading a conversation or when viewing a conversation list.

Table A.3

Message Commands	
KEYSTROKE(S)	TASK
c	Compose a new message
C	Compose a new message (in a new window)
r	Compose a reply to the current message
R	Compose a reply to the current message (in a new window)
a	Compose a reply to all recipients of the current message
A	Compose a reply to all recipients of the current message (in a new window)
f	Forward the current message
F	Forward the current message (in a new window)
Tab Enter	Send the current message (Internet Explorer only)
s	Add or remove a star from the current message
!	Mark the current message as spam, removing it from the message list
k	Go to the next newer message
j	Go to the next older message
u	Return to the conversation list (when viewing messages within a conversation)

Table A.4

Miscellaneous Commands	
KEYSTROKE(S)	TASK
Esc	Clear cursor from the current input field
/	Select the Search Mail text box

B

Advanced Search Operators

When performing a search in the Search Message box or creating a filter (Chapter 7), you can use the *advanced search operators* in **Table A.1** to set specific search criteria. (When creating a filter, advanced search operators can be entered in the Has the words box.)

You can combine advanced search operators (*contract from:suzie*) to create an And search in which multiple criteria must be satisfied. (*Note:* There is no AND operator. Whenever you search for two or more words, you are automatically performing an And search.)

To create an either/or search, use the OR advanced search operator (*from:suzie OR from:susan*).

Table A.1

Advanced Search Operators*		
OPERATOR	**EXPLANATION**	**EXAMPLES**
from:	Search for a message sender	**from:steve** (messages with Steve as sender)
to:	Search for a message recipient	**to:susan** (messages with Susan as recipient)
cc: or bcc:	Search for messages with particular recipients in the cc: or bcc: line	**cc:nancy** (messages with Nancy as a cc: recipient) **bcc:mark** (messages with Mark as a bcc: recipient)
subject:	Search for words in the Subject line	**subject:book** (messages with *book* in the Subject)
has:attachment	Search for messages with one or more attached files	**from:suzie has:attachment** (messages from Suzie with an attached file)
filename:	Search for a message with an attachment that has a given filename or is of a particular file type	**filename:budget.xls** (message with an attached Excel worksheet named budget.xls) **filename:jpg** (messages with attached JPEG graphic file)
after: or before:	Search by message date (entered in *yyyy/mm/dd* format)	**after:2005/10/15** (messages sent after Oct. 15, 2005) **after:2005/11/30 before:2006/01/01** (messages sent in the month of December, 2005)
label:	Search for messages with a given label	**label:peachpit** (messages with the label *peachpit*)
is:starred, is:read, or is:unread	Search for messages by status (marked with a star, read, or unread)	**from:Ken is:starred** (all starred messages from Ken) **is:unread** (all unread messages) **from:nancy is:read** (all previously read messages received from Nancy)
in:inbox, in:spam, or in:trash	Search for a message in a specific Gmail location	**subject:mortgage in:spam** (messages in Spam with the word *mortgage* in the Subject line)
in:anywhere	Search for messages anywhere in your account, including in Spam or Trash (normally excluded)	**from:sam in:anywhere** (message from Sam in any location, including Spam and Trash)
" " (quotes)	Search for an exact text string	**subject:"gmail test"** (messages with these two words together in the Subject line)
()	To perform an AND search using multiple words, enclose the words in parentheses	**subject:(FileMaker book)** (messages that contain both *FileMaker* and *book* anywhere in the Subject line) **from:Steve (FileMaker book)** (messages from Steve that contain both *FileMaker* and *book* anywhere in the text)
OR	Find messages that satisfy either of two criteria (note that OR must be in capital letters)	**subject:dog OR from:kennels.com** (messages with the word *dog* in the Subject or from the *kennels.com* domain **from:suzie OR from:cliff** (messages from Suzie or Cliff)
- (hyphen)	Exclude messages that contain this word	**FileMaker -book** (messages that contain the word *FileMaker*, but not the word *book*)

*Many of the advanced search operators are directly accessible by clicking the Show search options link.

INDEX

D

E

F

G

H

I

J

K

L

M

Visit Peachpit on the Web at www.peachpit.com

- Read the latest articles and download timesaving tipsheets from best-selling authors such as Scott Kelby, Robin Williams, Lynda Weinman, Ted Landau, and more!

- Join the Peachpit Club and save 25% off all your online purchases at peachpit.com every time you shop—plus enjoy free UPS ground shipping within the United States.

- Search through our entire collection of new and upcoming titles by author, ISBN, title, or topic. There's no easier way to find just the book you need.

- Sign up for newsletters offering special Peachpit savings and new book announcements so you're always the first to know about our newest books and killer deals.

- Did you know that Peachpit also publishes books by Apple, New Riders, Adobe Press, Macromedia Press and palmOne Press? Swing by the Peachpit family section of the site and learn about all our partners and series.

- Got a great idea for a book? Check out our About section to find out how to submit a proposal. You could write our next best-seller!

You'll find all this and more at www.peachpit.com. Stop by and take a look today!